PHILOSOPHY OF PUNISHMENT

Contemporary Issues in Philosophy

Series Editors

Robert M. Baird

Stuart E. Rosenbaum

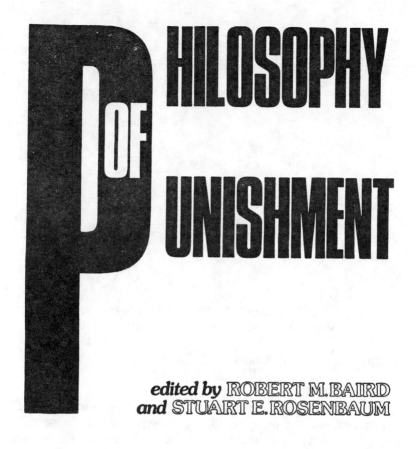

PHILOSOPHY OF PUNISHMENT

edited by ROBERT M. BAIRD
and STUART E. ROSENBAUM

PROMETHEUS BOOKS • AMHERST, NEW YORK

Published 1988 by Prometheus Books
59 John Glenn Drive, Amherst, New York 14228-2197

Library of Congress Cataloging-in-Publication Data

Philosophy of punishment/edited by Robert M. Baird and Stuart E.
    Rosenbaum
        p. cm.—(Contemporary issues in philosophy)
    Bibliography: p.
    ISBN 0-87975-417-6 (pbk.)
        1. Punishment. 2. Capital punishment. I. Baird, Robert M.,
1937-   . II. Rosenbaum. Stuart E. III. Series.
HV 8675.P53   1987   87-32718
364.6'01—dc 19   CIP

Printed in the United States of America

Contents

PART TWO: CAPITAL PUNISHMENT

Introduction

Ideas of punishment appear in different contexts: parents punish their children; boxers punish their opponents; armies punish their enemies; and judges and juries punish criminals. The most philosophically interesting idea of punishment is suggested by the last example. When judges and juries find criminals guilty and sentence them to suffer some penalty, the punishment is socially and legally institutionalized. In this case the question of justification becomes critical. Is punishment (any punishment) warranted or justified such that society may systematically impose suffering and deprivation on some of its members?

Other ideas of punishment do not convey this same puzzlement over justification. When parents punish their children, they impose suffering in virtue of a relationship of special responsibility for their offspring; when a boxer punishes his opponent, there is a special "game situation" in which he properly inflicts suffering of a specific kind; when an army punishes its enemy, all normal societal contexts have been replaced by a survival situation in which one must either impose destructive force on another or be its recipient. The idea that a society could institutionalize the imposition of suffering, deprivation, or death poses a distinct philosphical problem: What justifies such an institution?

To pose the question of justification one need not assume that the institution of punishment cannot be justified (and so perhaps ought to be abandoned), but it at least presents such a possibility. In any case, questions about the source and the nature of justifications for this customary social practice are quite compelling, and they are addressed by the essays in Part One of this volume. Part Two focuses on the issue of capital punishment, an extreme form of deprivation imposed only on individuals convicted of the most grievous crimes.

Two ostensibly opposed positions, retributivism and utilitarianism, have emerged as independent efforts to justify punishment. The retributivist maintains that punishment is simply what one deserves for having broken the law. This view is well encapsulated by the ancient Latin phrase *lex talionis,* or "an eye for an eye." For the retributivist, punishment is inherently justified in the act of law-breaking. The same reasoning that supports punishing a child for punching a younger sibling and taking his candy carries over to those who violate another by stealing from him. The child's inappropriate treatment of his sibling and the thief's violation of his victim are actions that, by their very nature, deserve punishment. The explication of this position is complex, but one plausible account is offered by Walter Berns in "The Morality of Anger."

One potential problem with the retributivist view is that it appears to justify punishment even when the punishment would have highly unfortunate (e.g., counterproductive) consequences. A man may be conscience-stricken about the plight of his family, who have been without food for three days. As a result he may decide to steal a loaf of bread from a wealthy neighbor. The retributivist view may justify imprisoning the man for theft even though the punishment may leave his family without support or the possibility of relief.

The utilitarian position seeks to avoid the difficulties of retributivism. Some utilitarians argue that penalties should be imposed only when to do so would be likely to result in more desirable consequences than not doing so. More than simply law-breaking is required to justify punishment. But why should the guilty be punished? Why is it permissible to inflict pain on one who has caused another suffering? Many utilitarians maintain that it is only because doing so has socially desirable consequences. In the case of the conscience-stricken man who steals bread to feed his family, a utilitarian might find punishment unjustified because of the undesirable consequences for the man's family. It is possible that the family might be more severely disadvantaged by his imprisonment than the wealthy neighbor was by the theft. For such a utilitarian, these consequences might mean that the punishment is unjustified; for the retributivist, such consequences are not relevant to the justification of the punishment. Although most utilitarians agree that inflicting pain or suffering on an individual is usually wrong, many would also agree that it is permissible when the desirable consequences more than offset the evil of imposing suffering.

Utilitarians usually emphasize two desirable consequences of punishment. The first is its *deterrent effect.* Punishment is socially valuable because it deters the criminal from repeating his act and may also deter others from engaging in similar acts. The example of one criminal suffering imprisonment for his deed may make others reluctant to commit similar crimes. Another socially desirable consequence of punishment is reform of the criminal. Since he behaved in a destructive and antisocial way, the criminal must be redirected. Punishment may change the person so that he no longer desires to thwart the social order by acts that violate the legitimate wants and needs of others. When the child is punished for inappropriate treatment of younger siblings, one result may be that he is no longer inclined to behave in such ways. Likewise, punishing the criminal may similarly change his inclinations to criminal behavior.

Critics of utilitarianism argue that awkward results follow from seeking to justify punishment in terms of its desirable consequences. They suggest that if the utilitarian is to remain consistent in his view, then he must maintain that sometimes innocent persons should be punished and at times the guilty should not be. If punishing a guilty person would yield worse results than not punishing him, then punishment would not be justified. On the other hand, if punishing an innocent person would yield better results than any alternative action, then such punishment would be justified. In an extreme case, law enforcement authorities may feel a need simply to arrest and punish any plausible suspect, even though they have no evidence suggesting that the suspect is in fact guilty. Some serious, perhaps gruesome, crime might, if unsolved, undermine public confidence in authority and perhaps even encourage potential criminals. The sacrifice of an innocent to avoid these bad results may sometimes appear justified by the utilitarian view.

Utilitarians might reply to this criticism by distinguishing between justifying the institution of punishment and justifying a particular act enjoined by the institution. It is the social institution of punishment whose justification is supported by utilitarian considerations. Individual cases of criminal behavior are dealt with by the policies, procedures, and practices that constitute the institution, and specific justifications for the disposition of individual cases are supplied only within the context of that institution. Utilitarian considerations do not legitimately reach the individual case when questions of justification are involved. Hence, the institution of punishment, justified by utilitarian considerations, does not permit innocent persons to be sacrificed on utilitarian grounds.

This distinction may also appear to reconcile the apparent conflict between retributivist and utilitarian views. As suggested above, utilitarian considerations apply only when punishment is justified as a social institution. Consistent with this, one could still argue that a particular individual can be punished only for retributive reasons; that is, only if he or she deserves punishment as stipulated within the policies of the institution.

The opening essay by H. L. A. Hart first defines punishment and then proceeds to distinguish between justifying the institution of punishment and justifying the punishment of a particular individual. While one might legitimately appeal to retribution (the guilty deserve to be punished) in justifying the punishment of a given individual, it does not follow that the same kind of appeal can legitimately be used to justify the institution of punishment itself. J. D. Mabbott, on the other hand, appears to side with retribution both as a means of justifying the institution of punishment and as a means of deciding which individuals are to be punished.

This issue is further developed in John Rawls's well-known article "Two Concepts of Rules," where he distinguishes between justifying a practice—a whole system of rules governing behavior—and justifying a particular act falling under the practice. Rawls applies this distinction where utilitarian arguments are appropriate in justifying the practice or institution of punishment but where retributive arguments are needed to justify applying provisions of the institution to a particular case.

Karl Menninger, a noted psychiatrist, denies that punishment can be justified as a social institution. Arguing that punishment of criminals has failed to achieve desirable goals, Menninger maintains that the institution of punishment should be replaced by a therapeutic program of rehabilitation for those involved in antisocial behavior.

Richard Wasserstrom emphasizes the deterrent function of punishment. He challenges Menninger and others who propose to replace punishment with therapy. Such an approach, he argues, focuses only on preventing repeated criminal acts, ignoring entirely the goal of preventing the first offense; since the latter is a major goal of punishment and the threat of punishment, Menninger's view fails.

In the concluding essay of Part One, Herbert Morris sides with Wasserstrom against Menninger, arguing that humans have a right to punishment. On his view, such a right is involved in being a person who freely chooses, and the right to be treated as a free person is one of the most fundamental of all rights.

The vital issues surrounding the more specific question of capital punishment are a mirror image of the issues surrounding the question of punishment in general. In Part Two the debate again pits retributivists against utilitarians, with the former favoring capital punishment and the latter in opposition.

The initial selection by Walter Berns, "The Morality of Anger," expresses a retributivist perspective in defense of capital punishment. Berns finds justification for capital punishment in the legitimacy and the communal necessity of anger.

Jeffrey Reiman also acknowledges the legitimacy of the retributivist case; however, he asserts that this rationale for the death penalty can be satisfied by the lesser penalty of life imprisonment. Since the legitimate demand for retribution can be satisfied by a lesser penalty, Reiman believes that a very important utilitarian consideration emerges. Since our institutions not only reflect but also shape our attitudes and character, we should use these institutions to help shape a more civilized general social character. In Reiman's opinion, refusing to sanction the death penalty would contribute to the civilizing mission of our social institutions.

Stephen Nathanson objects to the death penalty on the ground that, intentionally or not, it is in fact applied in discriminatory ways. Blacks who murder whites are far more likely to have the death penalty imposed on them than are whites who murder blacks. Since the death penalty is inevitably applied in discriminatory ways, says Nathanson, it is unjust to apply it at all.

Ernest van den Haag is well known for his support of capital punishment. In the selection we have chosen, he is specifically replying to the arguments of both Reiman and Nathanson. (They in fact single out his defense of retributivism for critical treatment.)

The controversy surrounding the issue of capital punishment is especially important in the present social and political climate of America. After a long pause, executions are now once again becoming more common. In addition, new techniques of execution are being employed; lethal injection is now the method of choice in Texas. Controversy over the death penalty attracts and nourishes extremists. Consequently, it is important to become familiar with the issues and the rationale behind competing positions. It is also important for each of us to try to form and evaluate his or her own view.

The selections presented here should prove helpful. Not only do they provide a good representation of the competing views, but they make clear the need for independent critical thought in formulating a position on the issues. Individually and as a society we are challenged by these selections to arrive at a reasoned point of view. Is van den Haag's reply to Reiman and Nathanson, for example, adequate to defend his perspective on capital punishment? This particular question can be addressed in a number of ways, and we warmly invite the reader to become involved in the controversy. More generally, the reader is urged to become involved in the debate over the possibility of providing a justification for punishment.

Part One

The Justification for Punishment

Prolegomenon to the Principles of Punishment

H. L. A. Hart

General interest in the topic of punishment has never been greater than it is at present and I doubt if the public discussion of it has ever been more confused. The interest and the confusion are both in part due to relatively modern skepticism about two elements which have figured as essential parts of the traditionally opposed "theories" of punishment. On the one hand, the old Benthamite confidence in fear of the penalties threatened by the law as a powerful deterrent, has waned with the growing realization that the part played by calculation of any sort in anti-social behavior has been exaggerated. On the other hand a cloud of doubt has settled over the keystone of "retributive" theory. Its advocates can no longer speak with the old confidence that statements of the form "This man who has broken the law could have kept it" had a univocal or agreed meaning; or where skepticism does not attach to the *meaning* of this form of statement, it has shaken the confidence that we are generally able to distinguish the cases where a statement of this form is true from those where it is not.[1]

Yet quite apart from the uncertainty engendered by these fundamental doubts, which seem to call in question the accounts given of the efficacy, and the morality of punishment by all the old competing theories, the public utterances of those who conceive themselves to be expounding, as plain men for other plain men, orthodox or common-sense principles (untouched by modern psychological doubts) are uneasy. Their words often sound as if the authors had not fully grasped their meaning or did not intend the words to be taken quite literally. A glance at the parliamentary debates or the *Report of the Royal Commission on Capital Punishment*[2] shows that many are now troubled by the suspicion that the view that there is just one supreme value or objective (e.g. Deterrence, Retribution, or Reform) in terms of which *all* questions about the justification of punishment are to be answered, is somehow wrong; yet, from what is said on such occasions no clear account of what the different values or objectives are, or how they fit together in the justification of punishment, can be extracted.[3]

No one expects judges or statesmen occupied in the business of sending people to the gallows or prison, or in making (or unmaking) laws which enable this to be done, to have much time for philosophical discussion of the principles which make it morally tolerable to do these things. A judicial bench is not and should not be a professorial chair. Yet what is said in public debates about punishment by those specially concerned with it as judges or legislators is important. Few are likely to be more circumspect, and if what they say seems, as it often does, unclear, one-sided, and easily refutable by pointing to some aspect of things which they have overlooked, it is likely that in our inherited ways of talking or thinking about punishment there is some persistent drive toward an over-simplification of multiple issues which require separate consideration. To counter this drive what is most needed is *not* the simple admission that instead of a single value or aim (Deterrence, Retribution, Reform or any other) a plurality of different values and aims should be given as a conjunctive answer to some *single* question concerning the justification of punishment. What is needed is the realization that different principles (each of which may in a sense be called a "justification") are relevant at different points in any morally acceptable account of punishment. What we should look for are answers to a number of different questions such as: What justifies the general practice of punishment? To whom may punishment be applied? How severely may we punish? In dealing with these and other questions concerning punishment we should bear in mind that in this, as in most other social institutions, the pursuit of one aim may be qualified by or provide an opportunity, not to be missed, for the pursuit of others. Till we have developed this sense of the complexity of punishment (and this prolegomenon aims only to do this) we shall be in no fit state to assess the extent to which the whole institution has been eroded by, or needs to be adapted to, new beliefs about the human mind.

There is, I think, an analogy worth considering between the concept of punishment and that of property. In both cases we have to do with a social institution of which the centrally important form is a structure of *legal* rules, even if it would be dogmatic to deny the names of punishment or property to the similar though more rudimentary rule-regulated practices within groups such as a family, or a school, or in customary societies whose customs may lack some of the standard or salient features of law (e.g. legislation, organized sanctions, courts). In both cases we are confronted by a complex institution presenting different interrelated features calling for separate explanation; or, if the morality of the institution is challenged, for separate justification. In both cases failure to distinguish separate questions or attempting to answer them all by reference to a single principle ends in confusion. Thus in the case of property we should distinguish between the question of the *definition* of property, the question why and in what circumstance it is a *good* institution to maintain, and the questions in what ways individuals may become *entitled* to acquire property and *how much* they should be allowed to acquire. These we may call questions of *Definition, General Justifying Aim,* and *Distribution* with the last subdivided into questions of *Title* and *Amount.* It is salutary to take some classical exposition of the idea of property, say Locke's chapter "Of Property" in the *Second Treatise,*[4] and to observe how much darkness is spread by the use of a single notion (in this case "the labor of [a man's] body and the work of his hands") to answer all these different questions which press upon us when we reflect on the institution of property. In the case of punishment the beginning of wisdom (though by no means its end) is to distinguish similar questions and confront them separately.

[Concerning the definition of punishment] I shall simply draw upon the recent admirable work scattered through English philosophical[5] journals and add to it only an admonition of my own against the abuse of definition in the philosophical discussion of punishment. So with Mr. Benn and Professor Flew I shall define the standard or central case of "punishment" in terms of five elements:

(i) It must involve pain or other consequences normally considered unpleasant.
(ii) It must be for an offense against legal rules.
(iii) It must be of an actual or supposed offender for his offense.
(iv) It must be intentionally administered by human beings other than the offender.
(v) It must be imposed and administered by an authority constituted by a legal system against which the offense is committed.

In calling this the standard or central case of punishment I shall relegate to the position of substandard or secondary cases the following among many other possibilities:

(a) Punishments for breaches of legal rules imposed or administered otherwise than by officials (decentralized sanctions).

(b) Punishments for breaches of non-legal rules or orders (punishments in a family or school).

(c) Vicarious or collective punishment of some member of a social group for actions done by others without the former's authorization, encouragement, control or permission.

(d) Punishment of persons (otherwise than under [c]) who neither are in fact nor supposed to be offenders.

The chief importance of listing these substandard cases is to prevent the use of what I shall call the "definitional stop" in discussions of punishment. This is an abuse of definition especially tempting when use is made of conditions (ii) and (iii) of the standard case in arguing against the utilitarian claim that the practice of punishment is justified by the beneficial consequences resulting from the observance of the laws which it secures. Here the stock "retributive" argument[6] is: If *this* is the justification of punishment, why not apply it, when it pays to do so, to those innocent of any crime, chosen at random, or to the wife and children of the offender? And here the wrong reply is: *That,* by definition, would not be "punishment" and it is the justification of punishment which is in issue.[7] Not only will this definitional stop fail to satisfy the advocate of "Retribution," it would prevent us from investigating the very thing which modern skepticism most calls in question: namely the rational and moral status of our preference for a system of punishment under which measures painful to individuals are to be taken against them only when they have committed an offense. Why do we prefer this to other forms of social hygiene which we might employ to prevent anti-social behavior and which we do employ in special circumstances, sometimes with reluctance? No account of punishment can afford to dismiss this question with a definition.

Before we reach any question of justification we must identify a preliminary question to which the answer is so simple that the question may not appear worth asking; yet it is clear that some curious "theories" of punishment gain their only plausibility from ignoring it, and others from confusing it with other questions. This question is: Why are certain kinds of action forbidden by law and so made crimes or offenses? The answer is: To announce to society that these actions are not to be done and to secure that fewer of them are done. These are the common immediate aims of making any conduct a criminal offense and until we have laws made with these primary aims we shall lack the notion of a "crime" and so of a "criminal." Without recourse to the simple idea that the criminal law sets up, in its rules, standards of behavior to encourage certain types of conduct and discourage others we cannot distinguish a punishment in the form of a fine from a tax on a course of conduct.[8] This indeed is one grave objection to those theories of law which in the interests of simplicity or uniformity obscure the distinction between primary laws setting standards for behavior and secondary laws specifying what officials must or may do when they are broken. Such theories insist that all legal rules are "really" directions to officials to exact "sanctions" under certain conditions, e.g. if people kill.[9] Yet only if we keep alive the distinction (which such theories thus obscure) between the primary objective of the law in encouraging or discouraging certain kinds of behavior, and its merely ancillary sanction or remedial steps, can we give sense to the notion of a crime or offense.

I shall not here criticize the intelligibility or consistency or adequacy of those theories that are united in denying that the practice of a system of punishment is justified by its beneficial consequences and claim instead that the main justification of the practice lies in the fact that when breach of the law involves moral guilt the application to the offender of the pain of punishment is itself a thing of value. A great variety of claims of this character, designating "Retribution" or "Expiation" or "Reprobation" as the justifying aim, fall in spite of differences under this rough general description. Though in fact I agree . . . in thinking that these all either avoid the question of justification altogether or are in spite of their protestations disguised forms of Utilitarianism, I shall assume that Retribution, defined simply as the application of the pains of punishment to an offender who is morally guilty, may figure among the conceivable justifying aims of a system of punishment. Here I shall merely insist that it is one thing to use the word Retribution *at this point* in an account of the principle of punishment in order to designate the General Justifying Aim of the system, and quite another to use it to secure that to the question "To whom may punishment be applied?" (the question of Distribution), the answer given is "Only to an offender for an offense." Failure to distinguish Retribution as a General Justifying Aim from retribution as the simple insistence that only those who have broken the law—and voluntarily broken it—may be punished, may be traced in many writers: even perhaps in Mr. J. D. Mabbott's[10] otherwise most illuminating essay. We shall distinguish the latter from Retribution in General Aim as "retribution in Distribution." Much confusing shadow-fighting between utilitarians and their opponents may be avoided if it is recognized that it is perfectly consistent to assert *both* that the General Justifying Aim of the practice of punishment is its beneficial consequences *and* that the pursuit of this General Aim should be qualified or restricted out of deference to principles of Distribution which require that punishment should be only of an offender for an offense. Conversely it does not in the least follow from the admission of the latter principle of retribution in Distribution that the General Justifying Aim of punishment is Retribution though of course Retribution in General Aim entails retribution in Distribution.

. . . *It* is worth observing that both the old fashioned Retributionist (in General Aim) and the most modern skeptic often make the same (and, I think, wholly mistaken) assumption that sense can only be made of the restrictive principle that punishment be applied only to an offender for an offense if the General Justifying Aim of the practice of punishment is Retribution. The skeptic consequently imputes to all systems of punishment (when they are restricted by the principle of retribution in Distribution) all the irrationality he finds in the idea of Retribution as a General Justifying Aim; conversely the advocates of the latter think the admission of retribution in Distribution is a refutation of the utilitarian claim that the social consequences of punishment are its Justifying Aim.

NOTES

1. See Barbara Wootton, *Social Science and Social Pathology* (1959), for a comprehensive modern statement of these doubts.

2. (1953) Cmd. 8932.

3. In the Lords' debate in July 1956 the Lord Chancellor agreed with Lord Denning that "the ultimate justification of any punishment is not that it is a deterrent but that it is the emphatic denunciation by the community of a crime" yet also said that "the real crux" of the question at issue is whether capital punishment is a uniquely effective deterrent. See 198 *H. L. Deb* (5th July) 576, 577, 596 (1956). In his article, "An Approach to the Problems of Punishment," *Philosophy* (1958), Mr. S. I. Benn rightly observes of Lord Denning's view that denunciation does not imply the deliberate imposition of suffering which is the feature needing justification (p. 328, n.1).

4. Chapter V.

5. K. Baier, "Is Punishment Retributive?" *Analysis* (1955), p. 25. A. Flew, "The Justification of Punishment," *Philosophy* (1954), p. 291. S. I. Benn, op. cit., pp. 325-6.

6. A. C. Ewing, *The Morality of Punishment*, D. J. B. Hawkins, *Punishment and Moral Responsibility* (The King's Good Servant, p. 92), J. D. Mabbott, "Punishment," *Mind* (1939), p. 152.

7. Mr. Benn seemed to succumb at times to the temptation to give "The short answer to the critics of utilitarian theories of punishment—that they are theories of *punishment* not of any sort of technique involving suffering" (op. cit., p. 332). He has since told me that he does not now rely on the definitional stop.

8. This generally clear distinction may be blurred. Taxes may be imposed to discourage the activities taxed though the law does not announce this as it does when it makes them criminal. Conversely fines payable for some criminal offenses because of a depreciation of currency become so small that they are cheerfully paid and offenses are frequent. They are then felt to be mere taxes because the sense is lost that the rule is meant to be taken seriously as a standard of behavior.

9. Cf. Kelsen, *General Theory of Law and State* (1945), pp. 30-33, 33-34, 143-4. "Law is the primary norm, which stipulates the sanction. . . ." (ibid. 61).

10. Op. cit. *supra* p. 5 n. 6. It is not always quite clear what he considers a "retributive" theory to be.

Punishment

J. D. Mabbott

I propose in this paper to defend a retributive theory of punishment and to reject absolutely all utilitarian considerations from its justification. I feel sure that this enterprise must arouse deep suspicion and hostility both among philosophers (who must have felt that the retributive view is the only moral theory except perhaps psychological hedonism which has been definitely destroyed by criticism) and among practical men (who have welcomed its steady decline in our penal practice).

The question I am asking is this. Under what circumstances is the punishment of some particular person justified and why? The theories of reform and deterrence which are usually considered to be the only alternatives to retribution involve well-known difficulties. These are considered fully and fairly in Dr. Ewing's book, *The Morality of Punishment*, and I need not spend long over them. The central difficulty is that both would on occasion justify the punishment of an innocent man, the deterrent theory if he were believed to have been guilty by those likely to commit the crime in future, and the reformatory theory if he were a bad man though not a criminal. To this may be added the point against the deterrent theory that it is the threat of punishment and not punishment itself which deters, and that when deterrence seems to depend on actual punishment, to implement the threat, it really depends on publication and may be achieved if men believe that punishment has occurred even if in fact it has not. As Bentham saw, for a Utilitarian apparent justice is everything, real justice is irrelevant.

Dr. Ewing and other moralists would be inclined to compromise with retribution in the face of the above difficulties. They would admit that one fact and one fact only can justify the punishment of this man, and

From J. D. Mabbott, "Punishment," *Mind* 48 (April 1939). Reprinted by permission of Oxford University Press.

that is a *past* fact, that he has committed a crime. To this extent reform and deterrence theories, which look only to the consequences, are wrong. But they would add that retribution can determine only *that* a man should be punished. It cannot determine how or how much, and here reform and deterrence may come in. Even Bradley, the fiercest retributionist of modern times, says "Having once the right to punish we may modify the punishment according to the useful and the pleasant, but these are external to the matter; they cannot give us a right to punish and nothing can do that but criminal desert." Dr. Ewing would maintain that the whole estimate of the amount and nature of a punishment may be effected by considerations of reform and deterrence. It seems to me that this is a surrender which the upholders of retribution dare not make. As I said above, it is publicity and not punishment which deters, and the publicity though often spoken of as "part of a man's punishment" is no more part of it than his arrest or his detention prior to trial, though both these may be also unpleasant and bring him into disrepute. A judge sentences a man to three years' imprisonment not to three years *plus* three columns in the press. Similarly with reform. The vision of the prison chaplain is not part of a man's punishment nor is the visit of Miss Fields or Mickey Mouse.

The truth is that while punishing a man and punishing him justly, it is possible to deter others, and also to attempt to reform him, and if these additional goods are achieved the total state of affairs is better than it would be with the just punishment alone. But reform and deterrence are not modifications of the punishment, still less reasons for it. A parallel may be found in the case of tact and truth. If you have to tell a friend an unpleasant truth you may do all you can to put him at his ease and spare his feelings as much as possible, while still making sure that he understands your meaning. In such a case no one would say that your offer of a cigarette beforehand or your apology afterwards are modifications of the truth still less reasons for telling it. You do not tell the truth in order to spare his feelings, but having to tell the truth you also spare his feelings. So Bradley was right when he said that reform and deterrence were "external to the matter," but therefore wrong when he said that they may "modify the punishment." Reporters are admitted to our trials so that punishments may become public and help to deter others. But the punishment would be no less just were reporters excluded and deterrence not achieved. Prison authorities may make it possible that a convict may become physically or morally better. They cannot ensure either result; and the punishment would still be just if the criminal took no advantage of their arrangements and their efforts failed. Some moralists see this and exclude these "extra" arrangements for deterrence and reform. They say that it must be the punishment *itself* which reforms and deters. But it is just my point that the punishment *itself* seldom reforms the criminal and never deters others. It is only "extra" arrangements which have any chance of achieving either result. As this is the central point of my paper, at the cost of labored repetition I would ask the upholders of reform and deterrence two questions. Suppose it could be shown that a particular criminal had not been improved by a punishment and also that no other would-be criminal had been deterred by it, would that prove that the punishment was unjust? Suppose it were discovered that a particular criminal had lived a much better life after his release and that many would-be criminals believing him to have been guilty were influenced by his fate, but yet that the "criminal" was punished for something he had never done, would these excellent results prove the punishment just?

It will be observed that I have throughout treated punishment as a purely legal matter. A "criminal" means a man who has broken a law, not a bad man; an "innocent" man is a man who has not broken the law in connection with which he is being punished, though he may be a bad man and have broken other laws. Here I dissent from most upholders of the retributive theory—from Hegel, from Bradley, and from Dr. Ross. They maintain that the essential connection is one between punishment and moral or social wrongdoing.

My fundamental difficulty with their theory is the question of *status.* It takes two to make a punishment, and for a moral or social wrong I can find no punisher. We may be tempted to say when we hear of some brutal action "that ought to be punished"; but I cannot see how there can be duties which are nobody's duties. If I see a man ill-treating a horse in a country where cruelty to animals is not a legal offense, and I say to him "I shall now punish you," he will reply, rightly, "What has it to do with you? Who made you a judge and a ruler over me?" I may have a duty to try to stop him and one way of stopping him may be to hit him, but another way may be to buy the horse. Neither the blow nor the price is a punishment. For a moral offense, God alone has the *status* necessary to punish the offender; and the theologians are becoming more and more doubtful whether even God has a duty to punish wrongdoing.

Dr. Ross would hold that not all wrongdoing is punishable, but only invasion of the rights of others; and in such a case it might be thought that the injured party has a right to punish. His right, however, is rather a right to reparation, and should not be confused with punishment proper.

This connection, on which I insist, between punishment and crime, not between punishment and moral or social wrong, alone accounts for some of our beliefs about punishment, and also meets many objections to the retributive theory as stated in its ordinary form. The first point on which it helps us is with regard to retrospective legislation. Our objection to this practice is unaccountable on reform and deterrence theories. For a man who commits a wrong before the date on which a law against it is passed, is as much in need of reform as a man who commits it afterwards; nor is deterrence likely to suffer because of additional punishments for the same offense. But the orthodox retributive theory is equally at a loss here, for if punishment is given for moral wrongdoing or for invasion of the rights of others, that immorality or invasion existed as certainly before the passing of the law as after it.

My theory also explains, where it seems to me all others do not, the case of punishment imposed by an authority who believes the law in question is a bad law. I was myself for some time disciplinary officer of a college whose rules included a rule compelling attendance at chapel. Many of those who broke this rule broke it on principle. I punished them. I certainly did not want to reform them; I respected their characters and their views. I certainly did not want to drive others into chapel through fear of penalties. Nor did I think there had been a wrong done which merited retribution. I wished I could have believed that I would have done the same myself. My position was clear. They had broken a rule; they knew it and I knew it. Nothing more was necessary to make punishment proper.

I know that the usual answer to this is that the judge enforces a bad law because otherwise law in general would suffer and good laws would be broken. The effect of punishing good men for breaking bad laws is that fewer bad men break good laws.

[*Excursus on Indirect Utilitarianism.* The above argument is a particular instance of a general utilitarian solution of all similar problems. When I am in funds and consider whether I should pay my debts or give the same amount to charity, I must choose the former because repayment not only benefits my creditor (for the benefit to him might be less than the good done through charity) but also upholds the general credit system. I tell the truth when a lie might do more good to the parties directly concerned, because I thus increase general trust and confidence. I keep a promise when it might do more immediate good to break it, because indirectly I bring it about that promises will be more readily made in future and this will outweigh the immediate loss involved. Dr. Ross has pointed out that the effect on the credit system of my refusal to pay a debt is greatly exaggerated. But I have a more serious objection of principle. It is that in all these cases the indirect effects do not result from my wrong action—my lie or defalcation or bad faith—but from the publication of these actions. If in any instance the breaking of the rule were to remain unknown then I could consider only the direct or immediate consequences. Thus in my "compulsory chapel" case I could have considered which of my culprits were law-abiding men generally and unlikely to break any other college rule. Then I could have sent for each of these separately and said "I shall let you off if you will tell no one I have done so." By these means the general keeping of rules would not have suffered. Would this course have been correct? It must be remembered that the proceedings need not deceive everybody. So long as they deceive would-be law-breakers the good is achieved.

As this point is of crucial importance and as it has an interest beyond the immediate issue, and gives a clue to what I regard as the true general nature of law and punishment, I may be excused for expanding and illustrating it by an example or two from other fields. Dr. Ross says that two men dying on a desert island would have duties to keep promises to each other even though their breaking them would not affect the future general confidence in promises at all. Here is certainly the same point. But as I find that desert-island morality always rouses suspicion among ordinary men I should like to quote two instances from my own experience which also illustrate the problem.

(i) A man alone with his father at his death promises him a private and quiet funeral. He finds later that both directly and indirectly the keeping of this promise will cause pain and misunderstanding. He can see no particular positive good that the quiet funeral will achieve. No one yet knows that he has made the promise nor need anyone ever know. Should he therefore act as though it had never been made?

(ii) A college has a fund given to it for the encouragement of a subject which is now expiring. Other expanding subjects are in great need of endowment. Should the authorities divert the money? Those who oppose the diversion have previously stood on the past, the promise. But one day one of them discovers the "real reason" for this slavery to a dead donor. He says "We must consider not only the value of this money for these purposes, since on all direct consequences it should be diverted at once. We must remember the effect of this diversion on the general system of benefactions. We know that benefactors like to endow special objects, and this act of ours would discourage such benefactors in future and leave learning worse off." Here again is the indirect utilitarian reason for choosing the alternative which direct utilitarianism would reject. But the immediate answer to this from the most ingenious member of the opposition was crushing and final. He said, "Divert the money but keep it dark." This is obviously correct. It is not the act of diversion which would diminish the stream of benefactions but the news of it reaching the ears of benefactors. Provided that no possible benefactor got to hear of it no indirect loss would result. But the justification of our action would depend entirely on the success of the measures for "keeping it dark." I remember how I felt and how others felt that whatever answer was right this result was certainly wrong. But it follows that indirect utilitarianism is wrong in all such cases. For its argument can always be met by "Keep it dark."]

The view, then, that a judge upholds a bad law in order that law in general should not suffer is indefensible. He upholds it simply because he has no right to dispense from punishment.

The connection of punishment with law-breaking and not with wrongdoing also escapes moral objections to the retributive theory as held by Kant and Hegel or by Bradley and Ross. It is asked how we can measure moral wrong or balance it with pain, and how pain can wipe out moral wrong. Retributivists have been pushed into holding that pain *ipso facto* represses the worse self and frees the better, when this is contrary to the vast majority of observed cases. But if punishment is not intended to measure or balance or negate moral wrong then all this is beside the mark. There is the further difficulty of reconciling punishment with repentance and with forgiveness. Repentance is the reaction morally appropriate to moral wrong and punishment added to remorse is an unnecessary evil. But if punishment is associated with law-breaking and not with moral evil the punisher is not entitled. to consider whether the criminal is penitent any more than he may consider whether the law is good. So, too, with forgiveness. Forgiveness is not appropriate to law-breaking. (It is noteworthy that when, in divorce cases, the law has to recognize forgiveness it calls it "condonation," which is symptomatic of the difference of attitude.) Nor is forgiveness appropriate to moral evil. It is appropriate to personal injury. No one has any right to forgive me except the person I have injured. No judge or jury can do so. But the person I have injured has no right to punish me. Therefore there is no clash between punishment and forgiveness since these two duties do not fall on the same person nor in connection with the same characteristic of my act. (It is the weakness of vendetta that it tends to confuse this clear line, though even there it is only by personifying the family that the injured party and the avenger are identified. Similarly we must guard against the plausible fallacy of personifying society and regarding the criminal as "injuring society," for then once more the old dilemma about forgiveness would be insoluble.) A clergyman friend of mine catching a burglar red-handed was puzzled about his duty. In the end he ensured the man's punishment by information and evidence, and at the same time showed his own forgiveness by visiting the man in prison and employing him when he came out. I believe any "good Christian" would accept this as representing his duty. But obviously if the punishment is thought of as imposed *by* the victim or *for* the injury or immorality then the contradiction with forgiveness is hopeless.

So far as the question of the actual punishment of any individual is concerned this paper could stop here. No punishment is morally retributive or reformative or deterrent. Any criminal punished for any one of these reasons is certainly unjustly punished. The only justification for punishing any man is that he has broken a law.

In a book which has already left its mark on prison administration I have found a criminal himself confirming these views. *Walls Have Mouths,* by W. F. R. Macartney, is prefaced, and provided with appendices to each chapter, by Compton Mackenzie. It is interesting to notice how the novelist maintains that the proper object of penal servitude should be reformation,[1] whereas the prisoner himself accepts the view I have set out above. Macartney says "To punish a man is to treat him as an equal. To be punished *for an offense against rules* is a sane man's right."[2] It is striking also that he never uses "injustice" to describe the brutality or provocation which he experienced. He makes it clear that there were only two types of prisoner who were *unjustly* imprisoned, those who were insane and not responsible for the acts for which they were punished[3] and those who were innocent and had broken no law.[4] It is irrelevant, as he rightly observes, that some of these innocent men were, like Steinie Morrison, dangerous and violent characters, who on utilitarian grounds might well have been restrained. That made their punishment no whit less unjust.[5] . . .

It will be objected that my original question "Why ought X to be punished?" is an illegitimate isolation of the issue. I have treated the whole set of circumstances as determined. X is a citizen of a state. About his citizenship, whether willing or unwilling, I have asked no questions. About the government, whether it is good or bad, I do not enquire. X has broken a law. Concerning the law, whether it is well-devised or not, I have not asked. Yet all these questions are surely relevant before it can be decided whether a particular punishment is just. It is the essence of my position that none of these questions is relevant. Punishment is a corollary of law-breaking by a member of the society whose law is broken. This is a static and an abstract view but I see no escape from it. Considerations of utility come in on two quite different issues. Should there be laws, and what laws should there be? As a legislator I may ask what general types of action would benefit the community and, among these, which can be "standardized" without loss, or should be standardized to achieve their full value. This, however, is not the primary question since particular laws may be altered or repealed. The choice which is the essential *prius* of punishment is the choice that there should be laws. This choice is not Hobson's. Other methods may be considered. A government might attempt to standardize certain modes of action by means of advice. It might proclaim its view and say "Citizens are requested" to follow this or that procedure. Or again it might decide to deal with each case as it arose in the manner most effective for the common welfare. Anarchists have wavered between these two alternatives and a third—that of doing nothing to enforce a standard of behavior but merely giving arbitrational decisions between conflicting parties, decisions binding only by consent.

I think it can be seen without detailed examination of particular laws that the method of law-making has its own advantages. Its orders are explicit and general. It makes behavior reliable and predictable. Its threat of punishment may be so effective as to make punishment unnecessary. It promises to the good citizen a certain security in his life. When I have talked to business men about some inequity in the law of liability they have usually said "Better a bad law than no law, for then we know where we are."

Someone may say I am drawing an impossible line. I deny that punishment is utilitarian; yet now I say that punishment is a corollary of law and we decide whether to have laws and which laws to have on utilitarian grounds. And surely it is only this corollary which distinguishes any law from good advice or exhortation. This is a misunderstanding. Punishment is a corollary not of law but of law-breaking. Legislators do not *choose* to punish. They hope no punishment will be needed. Their laws would succeed even if no punishment occurred. The criminal makes the essential choice; he "brings it on himself." Other men obey the law because they see its order is reasonable, because of inertia, because of fear. In this whole area, and it may be the major part of the state, law achieves its ends without punishment. Clearly, then, punishment is not a corollary of law.

We may return for a moment to the question of amount and nature of punishment. It may be thought that this also is automatic. The law will include its own penalties and the judge will have no option. This, however, is again an initial choice of principle. If the laws do include their own penalties then the judge has no option. But the legislature might adopt a system which left complete or partial freedom to the judge, as we do except in the case of murder. Once again, what are the merits (regardless of particular laws, still more of particular cases) of fixed penalties and variable penalties? At first sight it would seem that all the advantages are with the variable penalties; for men who have broken the same law differ widely in degree of wickedness and responsibility. When, however, we remember that punishment is not an attempt to balance moral guilt this advantage is diminished. But there are still degrees of responsibility; I do not mean degrees of freedom of will but, for instance, degrees of complicity in a crime. The danger of allowing complete freedom to the judicature in fixing penalties is not merely that it lays too heavy a tax on human nature but that it would lead to the judge expressing in his penalty the degree of his own moral aversion to the crime. Or he might tend on deterrent grounds to punish more heavily a crime which was spreading and for which temptation and opportunity were frequent. Or again on deterrent grounds he might "make examples" by punishing ten times as heavily those criminals who are detected in cases in which nine out of ten evade detection. Yet we should revolt from all such punishments if they involved punishing theft more heavily than blackmail or negligence more heavily than premeditated assault. The death penalty for sheep-stealing might have been defended on such deterrent grounds. But we should dislike equating sheep-stealing with murder. Fixed penalties enable us to draw these distinctions between crimes. It is not that we can say how much imprisonment is right for a sheep-stealer. But we can grade crimes in a rough scale and penalties in a rough scale, and keep our heaviest penalties for what are socially the most serious wrongs regardless of whether these penalties will reform the criminal or whether they are exactly what deterrence would require. The compromise of laying down maximum penalties and allowing judges freedom below these limits allows for the arguments on both sides.

To return to the main issue, the position I am defending is that it is essential to a legal system that the infliction of a particular punishment should *not* be determined by the good *that particular punishment* will do either to the criminal or to "society." In exactly the same way it is essential to a credit system that the repayment of a particular debt should not be determined by the good that particular payment will do. One may consider the merits of a legal system or of a credit system, but the acceptance of either involves the surrender of utilitarian considerations in particular cases as they arise. This is in effect admitted by Ewing in one place where he says "It is the penal system as a whole which deters and not the punishment of any individual offender."[6]

To show that the choice between a legal system and its alternatives is one we do and must make, I may quote an early work of Lenin in which he was defending the Marxist tenet that the state is bound to "wither away" with the establishment of a classless society. He considers the possible objection that some wrongs by man against man are not economic and therefore that the abolition of classes would not *ipso facto* eliminate crime. But he sticks to the thesis that these surviving crimes should not be dealt with by law and judicature. "We are not Utopians and do not in the least deny the possibility and inevitability of excesses by *individual persons,* and equally the need to suppress such excesses. But for this no special machine, no special instrument of repression is needed. This will be done by the armed nation itself as simply and as readily as any crowd of civilized people even in modern society parts a pair of combatants or does not allow a woman to be outraged."[7] This alternative to law and punishment has obvious demerits. Any injury not committed in the presence of the crowd, any wrong which required skill to detect or pertinacity to bring home would go untouched. The lynching mob, which is Lenin's instrument of justice, is liable to error and easily deflected from its purpose or driven to extremes. It must be a mob, for there is to be no "machine." I do not say that no alternative machine to ours could be devised but it does seem certain that the absence of all "machines" would be intolerable. An alternative machine might be based on the view that "society" is responsible for all criminality, and a curative and protective system developed. This is the system of Butler's "Erewhon" and something like it seems to be growing up in Russia except for cases of "sedition."

We choose, then, or we acquiesce in and adopt the choice of others of, a legal system as one of our instruments for the establishment of the conditions of a good life. This choice is logically prior to and independent of the actual punishment of any particular persons or the passing of any particular laws. The legislators choose particular laws within the framework of this predetermined system. Once again a small society may illustrate the reality of these choices and the distinction between them. A Headmaster launching a new school must explicitly make both decisions. First, shall he have any rules at all? Second, what rules shall he have? The first decision is a genuine one and one of great importance. Would it not be better to have an "honor" system, by which public opinion in each house or form dealt with any offense? (This is the Lenin method.) Or would complete freedom be better? Or should he issue appeals and advice? Or should he personally deal with each malefactor individually, as the case arises, in the way most likely to improve his conduct? I can well imagine an idealistic Headmaster attempting to run a school with one of these methods or with a combination of several of them and therefore without punishment. I can even imagine that with a small school of, say, twenty pupils all open to direct personal psychological pressure from authority and from each other, these methods involving no "rules" would work. The pupils would of course grow up without two very useful habits, the habit of having some regular habits and the habit of obeying rules. But I suspect that most Headmasters, especially those of large schools, would either decide at once, or quickly be driven, to realize that some rules were necessary. This decision would be "utilitarian" in the sense that it would be determined by consideration of consequences. The question "what rules?" would then arise and again the issue is utilitarian. What action must be regularized for the school to work efficiently? The hours of arrival and departure, for instance, in a day school. But the one choice which is now no longer open to the Headmaster is whether he shall punish those who break the rules. For if he were to try to avoid this he would in fact simply be returning to the discarded method of appeals and good advice. Yet the Headmaster does not decide to punish. The pupils make the decision there. He decides actually to have rules and to threaten, but only hypothetically, to punish. The one essential condition which makes actual punishment just is a condition he *cannot* fulfill—namely that a rule should be broken.

I shall add a final word of consolation to the practical reformer. Nothing that I have said is meant to counter any movement for "penal reform" but only to insist that none of these reforms have anything to do with punishment. The only type of reformer who can claim to be reforming the system of punishment is a follower of Lenin or or Samuel Butler who is genuinely attacking the *system* and who believes there should be no laws and no punishments. But our great British reformers have been concerned not with punishment but with its accessories. When a man is sentenced to imprisonment he is not sentenced also to partial starvation, to physical brutality, to pneumonia from damp cells and so on. And any movement which makes his food sufficient to sustain health, which counters the permanent tendency to brutality on the part of his warders, which gives him a dry or even a light and well-aired cell, is pure gain and does not touch the theory of punishment. Reformatory influences and prisoners' aid arrangements are also entirely unaffected by what I have said. I believe myself that it would be best if all such arrangements were made optional for the prisoner, so as to leave him in these cases a freedom of choice which would make it clear that they are not part of his punishment. If it is said that every such reform lessens a man's punishment, I think that is simply muddled thinking which, if it were clear, would be mere brutality. For instance, a prisoners' aid society is said to lighten his punishment, because otherwise he would suffer not merely imprisonment but also unemployment on release. But he was sentenced to imprisonment, not imprisonment *plus* unemployment. If I promise to help a friend and through special circumstances I find that keeping my promise will involve upsetting my day's work, I do not say that I really promised to help him and to ruin my day's work. And if another friend carries on my work for me I do not regard him as carrying out part of my promise, nor as stopping me from carrying it out myself. He merely removes an indirect and regrettable consequence of my keeping my promise. So with punishment. The Prisoners' Aid Society does not alter a man's punishment nor diminish it, but merely removes an indirect and regrettable consequence of it. And anyone who thinks that a criminal cannot make this distinction and will regard all the inconvenience that comes to him as punishment, need only talk to a prisoner or two to find how sharply they resent these wanton additions to a punishment which by itself they will accept as just. Macartney's chapter on "Food" in the book quoted above is a good illustration of this point, as are also his comments on Clayton's administration. "To keep a man in prison for many years at considerable expense and then to free him charged to the eyes with uncontrollable venom and hatred generated by the treatment he has received in gaol, does not appear to be sensible." Clayton "endeavored to send a man out of prison in a reasonable state of mind. 'Well, I've done my time. They were not too bad to me. Prison is prison and not a bed of roses. Still they didn't rub it in. . . .'"[8] This "reasonable state of mind" is one in which a prisoner on release feels he has been punished but not *additionally* insulted or ill-treated. I feel convinced that penal reformers would meet with even more support if they were clear that they were *not* attempting to alter the system of punishment but to give its victims "fair play." We have no more right to starve a convict than to starve an animal. We have no more right to keep a convict in a Dartmoor cell "down which the water trickles night and day"⁵ than we have to keep a child in such a place. If our reformers really want to alter the system of punishment, let them come out clearly with their alternative and preach, for instance, that no human being is responsible for any wrongdoing, that all the blame is on society, that curative or protective measures should be adopted, forcibly if necessary, as they are with infection or insanity. Short of this let them admit that the essence of prison is deprivation of liberty for the breaking of law, and that deprivation of food or of health or of books is unjust. And if our sentimentalists cry "coddling of prisoners," let us ask them also to come out clearly into the open and incorporate whatever starvation and disease and brutality they think necessary *into the sentences they propose.*[10] If it is said that some prisoners will prefer such reformed prisons, with adequate food and aired cells, to the outer world, we may retort that their numbers are probably not greater than those of the masochists who like to be flogged. Yet we do not hear the same "coddling" critics suggest abolition of the lash on the grounds that some criminals may like it. Even if the abolition from our prisons of all maltreatment other than that imposed by law results in a few down-and-outs breaking a window (as O. Henry's hero did) to get a night's lodging, the country will lose less than she does by her present method of sending out her discharged convicts "charged with venom and hatred" because of the additional and uncovenanted "rubbing it in" which they have received.

I hope I have established both the theoretical importance and the practical value of distinguishing between penal reform as we know and approve it—that reform which alters the accompaniments of punishment without touching its essence—and those attacks on punishment itself which are made not only by reformers who regard criminals as irresponsible and in need of treatment, but also by every judge who announces that he is punishing a man to deter others or to protect society, and by every juryman who is moved to his decision by the moral baseness of the accused rather than by his legal guilt.

NOTES

1. P. 97.
2. P. 165. My italics.
3. Pp. 165-66.
4. P. 298.
5. P. 301.
6. *The Morality of Punishment*, p. 66.
7. *The State and Revolution* (Eng. Trans.), p. 93. Original italics.

8. P. 152.

9. *Op. cit.,* p. 258.

10. "One of the minor curiosities of jail life was that they quickly provided you with a hundred worries which left you no time or energy for worrying about your sentence, long or short. . . . Rather as if you were thrown into a fire with spikes in it, and the spikes hurt you so badly that you forget about the fire. But then your punishment would *be* the spikes not the fire. Why did they pretend it was only the fire, when they knew very well about the spikes?" (From *Lifer,* by Jim Phelan, p. 40.)

Two Concepts of Rules

John Rawls

In this paper I want to show the importance of the distinction between justifying a practice[1] and justifying a particular action falling under it, and I want to explain the logical basis of this distinction and how it is possible to miss its significance. While the distinction has frequently been made,[2] and is now becoming commonplace, there remains the task of explaining the tendency either to overlook it altogether, or to fail to appreciate its importance.

To show the importance of the distinction I am going to defend utilitarianism against those objections which have traditionally been made against it in connection with punishment. . . . I hope to show that if one uses the distinction in question then one can state utilitarianism in a way which makes it a much better explication of our considered moral judgments than these traditional objections would seem to admit.[3] Thus the importance of the distinction is shown by the way it strengthens the utilitarian view regardless of whether that view is completely defensible or not.

To explain how the significance of the distinction may be overlooked, I am going to discuss two conceptions of rules. One of these conceptions conceals the importance of distinguishing between the justification of a rule or practice and the justification of a particular action falling under it. The other conception makes it clear why this distinction must be made and what is its logical basis.

The subject of punishment, in the sense of attaching legal penalties to the violation of legal rules, has always been a troubling moral question. The trouble about it has not been that people disagree as to whether or not punishment is justifiable. Most people have held that, freed from certain abuses, it is an acceptable institution. Only a few have rejected

From *The Philosophical Review* (1955): 3-13. Reprinted by permission of the publisher and the author.

punishment entirely, which is rather surprising when one considers all that can be said against it. The difficulty is with the justification of punishment: various arguments for it have been given by moral philosophers, but so far none of them has won any sort of general acceptance; no justification is without those who detest it. I hope to show that the use of the aforementioned distinction enables one to state the utilitarian view in a way which allows for the sound points of its critics.

For our purposes we may say that there are two justifications of punishment. What we may call the retributive view is that punishment is justified on the grounds that wrongdoing merits punishment. It is morally fitting that a person who does wrong should suffer in proportion to his wrongdoing. That a criminal should be punished follows from his guilt, and the severity of the appropriate punishment depends on the depravity of his act. The state of affairs where a wrongdoer suffers punishment is morally better than the state of affairs where he does not; and it is better irrespective of any of the consequences of punishing him.

What we may call the utilitarian view holds that on the principle that bygones are bygones and that only future consequences are material to present decisions, punishment is justifiable only by reference to the probable consequences of maintaining it as one of the devices of the social order. Wrongs committed in the past are, as such, not relevant considerations for deciding what to do. If punishment can be shown to promote effectively the interest of society it is justifiable, otherwise it is not.

I have stated these two competing views very roughly to make one feel the conflict between them: one feels the force of *both* arguments and one wonders how they can be reconciled. From my introductory remarks it is obvious that the resolution which I am going to propose is that in this case one must distinguish between justifying a practice as a system of rules to be applied and enforced, and justifying a particular action which falls under these rules; utilitarian arguments are appropriate with regard to questions about practices, while retributive arguments fit the application of particular rules to particular cases.

We might try to get clear about this distinction by imagining how a father might answer the question of his son. Suppose the son asks, "Why was *J* put in jail yesterday?" The father answers, "Because he robbed the bank at *B*. He was duly tried and found guilty. That's why he was put in jail yesterday." But suppose the son had asked a different question, namely, "Why do people put other people in jail?" Then the father might answer, "To protect good people from bad people" or "To stop people from doing things that would make it uneasy for all of us; for otherwise we wouldn't be able to go to bed at night and sleep in peace." There are two very different questions here. One question emphasizes the proper name: it asks why *J* was punished rather than someone else, or it asks what he was punished for. The other question asks why we have the institution of punishment: why do people punish one another rather than, say, always forgiving one another?

Thus the father says in effect that a particular man is punished, rather than some other man, because he is guilty, and he is guilty because he broke the law (past tense). In his case the law looks back, the judge looks back, the jury looks back, and a penalty is visited upon him for something he did. That a man is to be punished, and what his punishment is to be, is settled by its being shown that he broke the law and that the law assigns that penalty for the violation of it.

On the other hand we have the institution of punishment itself, and recommend and accept various changes in it, because it is thought by the (ideal) legislator and by those to whom the law applies that, as a part of a system of law impartially applied from case to case arising under it, it will have the consequence, in the long run, of furthering the interests of society.

One can say, then, that the judge and the legislator stand in different positions and look in different directions: one to the past, the other to the future. The justification of what the judge does, *qua* judge, sounds like the retributive view; the justification of what the (ideal) legislator does, *qua* legislator, sounds like the utilitarian view. Thus both views have a point (this is as it should be since intelligent and sensitive persons have been on both sides of the argument); and one's initial confusion disappears once one sees that these views apply to persons holding different offices with different duties, and situated differently with respect to the system of rules that make up the criminal law.[5]

One might say, however, that the utilitarian view is more fundamental since it applies to a more fundamental office, for the judge carries out the legislator's will so far as he can determine it. Once the legislator decides to have laws and to assign penalties for their violation (as things are there must be both the law and the penalty) an institution is set up which involves a retributive conception of particular cases. It is part of the concept of the criminal law as a system of rules that the application and enforcement of these rules in particular cases should be justifiable by arguments of a retributive character. The decision whether or not to use law rather than some other mechanism of social control, and the decision as to what laws to have and what penalties to assign, may be settled by utilitarian arguments; but if one decides to have laws then one has decided on something whose working in particular cases is retributive in form.[6]

The answer, then, to the confusion engendered by the two views of punishment is quite simple: one distinguishes two offices, that of the judge and that of the legislator, and one distinguishes their different stations with respect to the system of rules which make up the law; and then one notes that the different sorts of considerations which would usually be offered as reasons for what is done under the cover of these offices can be paired off with the competing justifications of punishment. One reconciles the two views by the time-honored device of making them apply to different situations.

But can it really be this simple? Well, this answer allows for the apparent intent of each side. Does a person who advocates the retributive view necessarily advocate, as an *institution,* legal machinery whose essential purpose is to set up and preserve a correspondence between moral turpitude and suffering? Surely not.[7] What retributionists have rightly insisted upon is that no man can be punished unless he is guilty, that is, unless he has broken the law. Their fundamental criticism of the utilitarian account is that, as they interpret it, it sanctions an innocent person's being punished (if one may call it that) for the benefit of society.

On the other hand, utilitarians agree that punishment is to be inflicted only for the violation of law. They regard this much as understood from the concept of punishment itself.[8] The point of the utilitarian account concerns the institution as a system of rules: utilitarianism seeks to limit its use by declaring it justifiable only if it can be shown to foster effectively the good of society. Historically it is a protest against the indiscriminate and ineffective use of the criminal law.[9] It seeks to dissuade us from assigning to penal institutions the improper, if not sacrilegious, task of matching suffering with moral turpitude. Like others, utilitarians want penal institutions designed so that, as far as humanly possible, only those who break the law run afoul of it. They hold that no official should have discretionary power to inflict penalties whenever he thinks it for the benefit of society; for on utilitarian grounds an institution granting such power could not be justified.[10]

The suggested way of reconciling the retributive and the utilitarian justifications of punishment seems to account for what both sides have wanted to say. There are, however, two further questions which arise, and I shall devote the remainder of this section to them.

First, will not a difference of opinion as to the proper criterion of just law make the proposed reconciliation unacceptable to retributionists? Will they not question whether, if the utilitarian principle is used as the criterion, it follows that those who have broken the law are guilty in a way which satisfies their demand that those punished deserve to be punished? To answer this difficulty, suppose that the rules of the criminal law are justified on utilitarian grounds (it is only for laws that meet his criterion that the utilitarian can be held responsible). Then it follows that the actions which the criminal law specifies as offenses are such that, if they were tolerated, terror and alarm would spread in society. Consequently, retributionists can only deny that those who are punished deserve to be punished if they deny that such actions are wrong. This they will not want to do.

The second question is whether utilitarianism doesn't justify too much. One pictures it as an engine of justification which, if consistently adopted, could be used to justify cruel and arbitrary institutions. Retributionists may be supposed to concede that utilitarians *intend* to reform the law and to make it more humane; that utilitarians do not *wish* to justify any such thing as punishment of the innocent; and that utilitarians may appeal to the fact that punishment presupposes guilt in the sense that by punishment one understands an institution attaching penalties to the infraction of legal rules, and therefore that it is logically absurd to suppose that utilitarians in justifying *punishment* might also have justified punishment (if we may call it that) of the innocent. The real question, however, is whether the utilitarian, in justifying punishment, hasn't used arguments which commit him to accepting the infliction of suffering on innocent persons if it is for the good of society (whether or not one calls this punishment). More generally, isn't the utilitarian committed in principle to accepting many practices which he, as a morally sensitive person, wouldn't want to accept? Retributionists are inclined to hold that there is no way to stop the utilitarian principle from justifying too much except by adding to it a principle which distributes certain rights to individuials. Then the amended criterion is not the greatest benefit of society *simpliciter,* but the greatest benefit of society subject to the constraint that no one's rights may be violated. Now while I think that the classical utilitarians proposed a criterion of this more complicated sort, I do not want to argue that point here.[11] What I want to show is that there is *another* way of preventing the utilitarian principle from justifying too much, or at least of making it much less likely to do so: namely, by stating utilitarianism in a way which accounts for the distinction between the justification of an institution and the justification of a particular action falling under it.

I begin by defining the institution of punishment as follows: a person is said to suffer punishment whenever he is legally deprived of some of the normal rights of a citizen on the ground that he has violated a rule of law, the violation having been established by trial according to the due process of law, provided that the deprivation is carried out by the recognized legal authorities of the state, that the rule of law clearly specifies both the offense and the attached penalty, that the courts construe statutes strictly, and that the statute was on the books prior to the time of the offense.[12] This definition specifies what I shall understand by punishment. The question is whether utilitarian arguments may be found to justify institutions widely different from this and such as one would find cruel and arbitrary.

This question is best answered, I think, by taking up a particular accusation. Consider the following from Carritt:

. . . the utilitarian must hold that we are justified in inflicting pain always and only to prevent worse pain or bring about greater happiness. This, then, is all we need to consider in so-called punishment, which must be purely preventive. But if some kind of very cruel crime becomes common, and none of the criminals can be caught, it might be highly expedient, as an example, to hang an innocent man, if a charge against him could be so framed that he were universally thought guilty; indeed this would only fail to be an ideal instance of utilitarian 'punishment' because the victim himself would not have been so likely as a real felon to commit such a crime in the future; in all other respects it would be perfectly deterrent and therefore felicific.[13]

Carritt is trying to show that there are occasions when a utilitarian argument would justify taking an action which would be generally condemned; and thus that utilitarianism justifies too much. But the failure of Carritt's argument lies in the fact that he makes no distinction between the justification of the general system of rules which constitutes penal institutions and the justification of particular applications of these rules to particular cases by the various officials whose job it is to administer them. This becomes perfectly clear when one asks who the "we" are of whom Carritt speaks. Who is this who has a sort of absolute authority on particular occasions to decide that an innocent man shall be "punished" if everyone can be convinced that he is guilty? Is this person the legislator, or the judge, or the body of private citizens, or what? It is utterly crucial to know who is to decide such matters, and by what authority, for all of this must be written into the rules of the institution. Until one knows these things one doesn't know what the institution is whose justification is being challenged; and as the utilitarian principle applies to the institution one doesn't know whether it is justifiable on utilitarian grounds or not.

Once this is understood it is clear what the countermove to Carritt's argument is. One must describe more carefully what the *institution* is which his example suggests, and then ask oneself whether or not it is likely that having this institution would be for the benefit of society in the long run. One must not content oneself with the vague thought that, when it's a question of *this* case, it would be a good thing if *somebody* did something even if an innocent person were to suffer.

Try to imagine, then, an institution (which we may call "telishment") which is such that the officials set up by it have authority to arrange a trial for the condemnation of an innocent man whenever they are of the opinion that doing so would be in the best interests of society. The discretion of officials is limited, however, by the rule that they may not condemn an innocent man to undergo such an ordeal unless there is, at the time, a wave of offenses similar to that with which they charge him and telish him for. We may imagine that the officials having the discretionary authority are the judges of the higher courts in consultation with the chief of police, the minister of justice, and a committee of the legislature.

Once one realizes that one is involved in setting up an *institution,* one sees that the hazards are very great. For example, what check is there on the officials? How is one to tell whether or not their actions are authorized? How is one to limit the risks involved in allowing such systematic deception? How is one to avoid giving anything short of complete discretion to the authorities to telish anyone they like? In addition to these considerations, it is obvious that people will come to have a very different attitude towards their penal system when telishment is adjoined to it. They will be uncertain as to whether a convicted man has been punished or telished. They will wonder whether or not they should feel sorry for him. They will wonder whether the same fate won't at any time fall on them. If one pictures how such an institution would actually work, and the enormous risks involved in it, it seems clear that it would serve no useful purpose. A utilitarian justification for this institution is most unlikely.

It happens in general that as one drops off the defining features of punishment one ends up with an institution whose utilitarian justification is highly doubtful. One reason for this is that punishment works like a kind of price system: by altering the prices one has to pay for the performance of actions it supplies a motive for avoiding some actions and doing others. The defining features are essential if punishment is to work in this way; so that an institution which lacks these features, e.g., an institution which is set up to "punish" the innocent, is likely to have about as much point as a price system (if one may call it that) where the prices of things change at random from day to day and one learns the price of something after one has agreed to buy it.[14]

If one is careful to apply the utilitarian principle to the institution which is to authorize particular actions, then there is *less* danger of its justifying too much. Carritt's example gains plausibility by its indefiniteness and by its concentration on the particular case. His argument will only hold if it can be shown that there are utilitarian arguments which justify an institution whose publicly ascertainable offices and powers are such as to permit officials to exercise that kind of discretion in particular cases. But the requirement of having to build the arbitrary features of the particular decision into the institutional practice makes the justification much less likely to go through.

NOTES

1. I use the word "practice" throughout as a sort of technical term meaning any form of activity specified by a system of rules which defines offices, roles, moves, penalties, defenses, and so on, and which gives the activity its structure. As examples one may think of games and rituals, trials and parliaments.

2. The distinction is central to Hume's discussion of justice in *A Treatise of Human Nature*, bk. III, pt. II, esp. secs. 2-4. It is clearly stated by John Austin in the second lecture of *Lectures on Jurisprudence* (4th ed.; London, 1873), I, 116ff. (1st ed., 1832). Also it may be argued that J. S. Mill took it for granted in *Utilitarianism;* on this point cf. J. O. Urmson, "The Interpretation of the Moral Philosophy of J. S. Mill," *Philosophical Quarterly,* vol. III (1953). In addition to the arguments given by Urmson there are several clear statements of the distinction in *A System of Logic* (8th ed.; London, 1872), bk. VI, ch. xii, pars. 2, 3, 7. The distinction is fundamental to J. D. Mabbdfffffott's important paper, "Punishment," *Mind,* n.s., vol. XLVIII (April, 1939). More recently the distinction has been stated with particular emphasis by S. E. Toulmin in *The Place of Reason in Ethics* (Cambridge, 1950), see esp. ch. xi, where it plays a major part in his account of moral reasoning. Toulmin doesn't explain the basis of the distinction, nor how one might overlook its importance, as I try to in this paper, and in my review of his book (*Philosophical Review,* vol. LX [October, 1951]), as some of my criticisms show, I failed to understand the force of it. See also H. D. Aiken, "The Levels of Moral Discourse," *Ethics,* vol. LXII (1952), A. M. Quinton, "Punishment," *Analysis,* vol. XIV (June, 1954), and P. H. Nowell-Smith, *Ethics* (London, 1954), pp. 236-239, 271-273.

3. On the concept of explication see the author's paper *Philosophical Review,* vol. LX (April, 1951).

4. While this paper was being revised, Quinton's appeared; footnote 2 supra. There are several respects in which my remarks are similar to his. Yet as I consider some further questions and rely on somewhat different arguments, I have retained the discussion of punishment and promises together as two test cases for utilitarianism.

5. Note the fact that different sorts of arguments are suited to different offices. One way of taking the differences between ethical theories is to regard them as accounts of the reasons expected in different offices.

6. In this connection see Mabbott, *op. cit.,* pp. 163-164.

7. On this point see Sir David Ross, *The Right and the Good* (Oxford, 1930), pp. 57-60.

8. See Hobbes's definition of punishment in *Leviathan,* ch. xxviii; and Bentham's definition in *The Principle of Morals and Legislation,* ch. xii, par. 36, ch. xv, par. 28, and in *The Rationale of Punishment,* (London, 1830), bk. I, ch. i. They could agree with Bradley that: "Punishment is punishment only when it is deserved. We pay the penalty, because we owe it, and for no other reason; and if punishment is inflicted for any other reason whatever than because it is merited by wrong, it is a gross immorality, a crying injustice, an abominable crime, and not what it pretends to be." *Ethical Studies* (2nd ed.; Oxford, 1927),

pp. 26-27. Certainly by definition it isn't what it pretends to be. The innocent can only be punished by mistake; deliberate "punishment" of the innocent necessarily involves fraud.

9. Cf. Leon Radzinowicz, *A History of English Criminal Law: The Movement for Reform 1750-1833* (London, 1948), esp. ch. xi on Bentham.

10. Bentham discusses how corresponding to a punitory provision of a criminal law there is another provision which stands to it as an antagonist and which needs a name as much as the punitory. He calls it, as one might expect, the *anaetiosostic,* and of it he says: "The punishment of guilt is the object of the former one: the preservation of innocence that of the latter." In the same connection he asserts that it is never thought fit to give the judge the option of deciding whether a thief (that is, a person whom he believes to be a thief, for the judge's belief is what the question must always turn upon) should hang or not, and so the law writes the provision: "The judge shall not cause a thief to be hanged unless he have been duly convicted and sentenced in course of law" (*The Limits of Jurisprudence Defined,* ed. C. W. Everett [New York, 1945], pp. 238-239).

11. By the classical utilitarians I understand Hobbes, Hume, Bentham, J. S. Mill, and Sidgwick.

12. All these features of punishment are mentioned by Hobbes; cf. *Leviathan,* ch. xxviii.

13. *Ethical and Political Thinking* (Oxford, 1947), p. 65.

14. The analogy with the price system suggests an answer to the question how utilitarian considerations insure that punishment is proportional to the offense. It is interesting to note that Sir David Ross, after making the distinction between justifying a penal law and justifying a particular application of it, and after stating that utilitarian considerations have a large place in determining the former, still holds back from accepting the utilitarian justification of punishment on the grounds that justice requires that punishment be proportional to the offense, and that utilitarianism is unable to account for this. Cf. *The Right and the Good,* pp. 61-62. I do not claim that utilitarianism can account for this requirement as Sir David might wish, but it happens, nevertheless, that if utilitarian considerations are followed penalties will be proportional to offenses in this sense: the order of offenses according to seriousness can be paired off with the order of penalties according to severity. Also the absolute level of penalties will be as low as possible. This follows from the assumption that people are rational (i.e., that they are able to take into account the "prices" the state puts on actions), the utilitarian rule that a penal system should provide a motive for preferring the less serious offense, and the principle that punishment as such is an evil. All this was carefully worked out by Bentham in *The Principles of Morals and Legislation,* chs. xiii-xv.

Therapy, Not Punishment

Karl Menninger

Since ancient times criminal law and penology have been based upon what is called in psychology the pain-pleasure principle. There are many reasons for inflicting pain—to urge an animal to greater efforts, to retaliate for pain received, to frighten, or to indulge in idle amusement. Human beings, like all animals, tend to move away from pain and toward pleasure. Hence the way to control behavior is to reward what is "good" and punish what is "bad." This formula pervades our programs of childrearing, education, and social control of behavior.

With this concept three out of four readers will no doubt concur.

"Why, of course," they will say. "Only common sense. Take me for example. I know the speed limit and the penalty. Usually I drive moderately because I don't want to get a ticket. One afternoon I was in a hurry; I had an appointment, I didn't heed the signs. I did what I knew was forbidden and I got caught and received the punishment I deserved. Fair enough. It taught me a lesson. Since then I drive more slowly in that area. And surely people are deterred from cheating on their income taxes, robbing banks, and committing rape by the fear of punishment. Why, if we didn't have these crime road blocks we'd have chaos!"

This sounds reasonable enough and describes what most people think— *part of the time*. But upon reflection we all know that punishments and the threat of punishments do *not* deter *some* people from doing forbidden things. Some of them take a chance on not being caught, and this chance is a very good one, too, better than five to one for most crimes. Not even the fear of possible death, self-inflicted, deters some speedsters. Exceeding the speed limit is not really regarded as criminal behavior by most people, no matter how dangerous and self-destructive. It is the kind

---

Originally published as "Verdict Guilty—Now What?" *Harpers Magazine* (August 1959): 60-64. Reprinted by permission of the author.

of a "crime" which respectable members of society commit and condone. This is not the case with rape, bank-robbing, check-forging, vandalism, and the multitude of offenses for which the prison penalty system primarily exists. And from these offenses the average citizen, including the reader, is deterred by quite different restraints. For most of us it is our conscience, our self-respect, and our wish for the good opinion of our neighbors which are the determining factors in controlling our impulses toward misbehavior.

Today it is no secret that our official, prison-threat theory of crime control is an utter failure. Criminologists have known this for years. When pocket-picking was punishable by hanging, in England, the crowds that gathered about the gallows to enjoy the spectacle of an execution were particularly likely to have their pockets picked by skillful operators who, to say the least, were not deterred by the exhibition of "justice." We have long known that the perpetrators of most offenses are never detected; of those detected, only a fraction are found guilty and still fewer serve a "sentence." Furthermore, we are quite certain now that of those who do receive the official punishment of the law, many become firmly committed thereby to a continuing life of crime and a continuing feud with law enforcement officers. Finding themselves ostracized from society and blacklisted by industry they stick with the crowd they have been introduced to in jail and try to play the game of life according to this set of rules. In this way society skillfully converts individuals of borderline self-control into loyal members of the underground fraternity.

The science of human behavior has gone far beyond the common sense rubrics which dictated the early legal statutes. We know now that one cannot describe rape or bank-robbing or income-tax fraud simply as pleasure. Nor, on the other hand, can we describe imprisonment merely as pain. Slapping the hand of a beloved child as he reaches to do a forbidden act is utterly different from the institutionalized process of official punishment. The offenders who are chucked into our county and state and federal prisons are not anyone's beloved children; they are usually unloved children, grown-up physically but still hungry for human concern which they never got or never get in normal ways. So they pursue it in abnormal ways—abnormal, that is, from *our* standpoint.

WHY OUR CRIME THERAPY HAS FAILED

What might deter the reader from conduct which his neighbors would not like does not necessarily deter the grown-up child of vastly different background. The latter's experiences may have conditioned him to believe that the chances of winning by undetected cheating are vastly greater than the probabilities of fair treatment and opportunity. He knows about the official threats and the social disapproval of such acts. He knows about the hazards and the risks. But despite all this "knowledge," he becomes involved in waves of discouragement or cupidity or excitement or resentment leading to episodes of social offensiveness.

These episodes may prove vastly expensive both to him and to society. But sometimes they will have an aura of success. Our periodicals have only recently described the wealth and prominence for a time of a man described as a murderer. Konrad Lorenz, the great psychiatrist and animal psychologist, has beautifully described in geese what he calls a "triumph reaction." It is sticking out of the chest and flapping of the wings after an encounter with a challenge. All of us have seen this primitive biological triumph reaction—in some roosters, for example, in some businessmen and athletes and others—*and* in some criminals.

In general, though, the gains and goals of the social offender are not those which most men seek. Most offenders whom we belabor are not very wise, not very smart, not even very "lucky." It is not the successful criminal upon whom we inflict our antiquated penal system. It is the unsuccessful criminal, the criminal who really doesn't know how to commit crimes, and who gets caught. Indeed, until he is caught and convicted a man is technically not even called a criminal. The clumsy, the desperate, the obscure, the friendless, the defective, the diseased—these men who commit crimes that do not come off—are bad actors, indeed. But they are not the professional criminals, many of whom occupy high places. In some instances the crime is the merest accident or incident or impulse, expressed under unbearable stress. More often the offender is a persistently perverse, lonely, and resentful individual who joins the only group to which he is eligible—the outcasts and the anti-social.

And what do we do with such offenders? After a solemn public ceremony we pronounce them enemies of the people, and consign them for arbitrary periods to institutional confinement on the basis of laws written many years ago. Here they languish until time has ground out so many weary months and years. Then with a planlessness and stupidity only surpassed by that of their original incarceration they are dumped back upon society, regardless of whether any change has taken place in them for the better and with every assurance that changes have taken place in them for the worse. Once more they enter the unequal tussle with society. Proscribed for employment by most concerns, they are expected to invent a new way to make a living to survive without any further help from society.

Intelligent members of society are well aware that the present system is antiquated, expensive, and disappointing, and that we are wasting vast quantities of manpower through primitive methods of dealing with those who transgress the law. In 1917 the famous Wickersham report of the New York State Prison Survey Committee recommended the abolition of jails, the institution of diagnostic clearing houses or classification centers, the development of a diversified institutional system and treatment program, and the use of indeterminate sentences. *Forty-two years have passed.* How little progress we have made! In 1933 the American Psychiatric Association, the American Bar Association, and the American Medical Association officially and jointly recommended psychiatric service for every criminal and juvenile court to assist the court and prison and parole officers with all offenders.

That was twenty-six years ago! Have these recommendations been carried out anywhere in the United States? With few exceptions offenders continue to be dealt with according to old-time instructions, written by men now dead who knew nothing about the present offender, his past life, the misunderstandings accumulated by him, or the provocation given to him.

The sensible, scientific question is: What kind of treatment could be instituted that would deter him or be most likely to deter him? Some of these methods are well known. For some offenders who have the money or the skillful legal counsel or the good luck to face a wise judge go a different route from the prescribed routine. Instead of jail and deterioration, they get the sort of re-education and re-direction associated with psychiatric institutions and the psychiatric profession. Relatively few wealthy offenders get their "treatment" in jail. This does not mean that justice is to be bought, or bought off. But it does mean that some offenders have relatives and friends who *care* and who try to find the best possible solution to the problem of persistent misbehavior, which is NOT the good old jail-and-penitentiary and make-'em-sorry treatment. It is a reflection on the democratic ideals of our country that these better ways are so often—indeed, *usually*—denied to the poor, the friendless, and the ignorant.

SCIENCE VERSUS TRADITION

If we were to follow scientific methods, the convicted offender would be detained indefinitely pending a decision as to whether and how and when to reintroduce him successfully into society. All the skill and knowledge of modern behavioral science would be used to examine his personality assets, his liabilities and potentialities, the environment from which he came, its effects upon him, and his effects upon it.

Having arrived at some diagnostic grasp of the offender's personality, those in charge can decide whether there is a chance that he can be redirected into a mutually satisfactory adaptation to the world. If so, the most suitable techniques in education, industrial training, group administration, and psychotherapy should be selectively applied. All this may be best done extramurally or intramurally. It may require maximum "security" or only minimum "security." If, in due time, perceptible change occurs, the process should be expedited by finding a suitable spot in society and industry for him, and getting him out of prison control and into civil status (with parole control) as quickly as possible.

The desirability of moving patients out of institutional control swiftly is something which we psychiatrists learned the hard way, and recently. Ten years ago, in the state hospital I know best, the average length of stay was five years; today it is three months. Ten years ago few patients were discharged in under two years; today 90 per cent are discharged within the first year. Ten years ago the hospital was overcrowded; today it has eight times the turnover it used to have; there are empty beds and there is no waiting list.

But some patients do not respond to our efforts, and they have to remain in the hospital, or return to it promptly after a trial home visit. And if the *prisoner,* like some of the psychiatric patients, cannot be changed by genuine efforts to rehabilitate him, we must look *our* failure in the face, and provide for his indefinitely continued confinement, regardless of the technical reasons for it. This we owe society for its protection.

There will be some offenders about whom the most experienced are mistaken, both ways. And there will be some concerning whom no one knows what is best. There are many problems for research. But what I have outlined is, I believe, the program of modern penology, the program now being carried out in some degree in California and a few other states, and in some of the federal prisons.

This civilized program, which would save so much now wasted money, so much unused manpower, and so much injustice and suffering, is slow to spread. It is held back by many things—by the continued use of fixed sentences in many places; by unenlightened community attitudes toward the offender whom some want tortured; by the prevalent popular assumption that burying a frustrated individual in a hole for a short time will change his warped mind, and that when he is certainly worse, he should be released because his "time" has been served; by the persistent failure of the law to distinguish between crime as an accidental, incidental, explosive event, crime as a behavior pattern expressive of chronic unutterable rage and frustration, and crime as a business or elected way of life. Progress is further handicapped by the lack of interest in the subject on the part of lawyers, most of whom are proud to say that they are not concerned with criminal law. It is handicapped by the lack of interest on the part of members of my own profession. It is handicapped by the mutual distrust of lawyers and psychiatrists.

The infestation or devil-possession theory of mental disease is an outmoded, pre-medieval concept. Although largely abandoned by psychiatry, it steadfastly persists in the minds of many laymen, including, unfortunately, many lawyers.

On the other hand, most lawyers have no really clear idea of the way in which a psychiatrist functions or of the basic concepts to which he adheres. They cannot understand, for example, why there is no such thing (for psychiatrists) as "insanity." Most lawyers have no conception of the meaning or methods of psychiatric case study and diagnosis. They seem to think that psychiatrists can take a quick look at a suspect, listen to a few anecdotes about him, and thereupon be able to say, definitely, that the awful "it"—the dreadful miasma of madness, the loathsome affliction of "insanity"—is present or absent. Because we all like to please, some timid psychiatrists fall in with this fallacy of the lawyers and go through these preposterous antics.

AS THE PSYCHIATRIST SEES IT

It is true that almost any offender—like anyone else—when questioned for a short time, even by the most skillful psychiatrist, can make responses and display behavior patterns which will indicate that he is enough like the rest of us to be called "sane." But a barrage of questions is not a psychiatric examination. Modern scientific personality study depends upon various specialists—physical, clinical, and sociological as well as psychological. It takes into consideration not only static and presently observable factors, but dynamic and historical factors, and factors of environmental interaction and change. It also looks into the future for correction, re-education, and prevention.

Hence, the same individuals who appear so normal to superficial observation are frequently discovered in the course of prolonged, intensive scientific study to have tendencies regarded as "deviant," "peculiar," "unhealthy," "sick," "crazy," "senseless," "irrational," "insane."

But now you may ask, "Is it not possible to find such tendencies in any individual if one looks hard enough? And if this is so, if we are all a little crazy or potentially so, what is the essence of your psychiatric distinctions? Who is it that you want excused?"

And here is the crux of it all. We psychiatrists don't want *anyone* excused. In fact, psychiatrists are much more concerned about the protection of the public than are the lawyers. I repeat; psychiatrists don't want anyone excused, certainly not anyone who shows antisocial tendencies. We consider them all responsible, which lawyers do not. And we want the prisoner to take on that responsibility, or else deliver it to someone who will be concerned about the protection of society and about the prisoner, too. We don't want anyone excused, but neither do we want anyone stupidly disposed of, futilely detained, or prematurely released. We don't want them tortured, either sensationally with hot irons or quietly by long-continued and forced idleness. In the psychiatrist's mind nothing should be done in the name of punishment, though he is well aware that the offender may regard either the diagnostic procedure or the treatment or the detention incident to the treatment as punitive. But this is in *his* mind, not in the psychiatrist's mind. And in our opinion it should not be in the public's mind, because it is an illusion.

It is true that we psychiatrists consider that all people have potentialities for antisocial behavior. The law assumes this, too. Most of the time most people control their criminal impulses. But for various reasons and under all kinds of circumstances some individuals become increasingly disorganized or demoralized, and then they begin to be socially offensive. The man who does criminal things is less convincingly disorganized than the patient who "looks" sick, because the former more nearly resembles the rest of us, and seems to be indulging in acts that we have struggled with and controlled. So we get hot under the collar about the one and we call him "criminal" whereas we pityingly forgive the other and call him "lunatic." But a surgeon uses the same principles of surgery whether he is dealing with a "clean" case, say some cosmetic surgery on a face, or a "dirty" case which is foul-smelling and offensive. What we are after is results and the emotions of the operator must be under control. Words like "criminal" and "insane" have no place in the scientific vocabulary any more than pejorative adjectives like "vicious," "psychopathic," "bloodthirsty," etc. The need is to find all the *descriptive* adjectives that apply to the case, and this is a scientific job—not a popular exercise in name-calling. Nobody's insides are very beautiful; and in the cases that require social control there has been a great wound and some of the insides are showing.

Intelligent judges all over the country are increasingly surrendering the onerous responsibility of deciding in advance what a man's conduct will be in a prison and how rapidly his wicked impulses will evaporate there. With more use of the indeterminate sentence and the establishment of scientific diagnostic centers, we shall be in a position to make progress in the science of *treating* antisocial trends. Furthermore, we shall get away from the present legal smog that hangs over the prisons, which lets us detain with heartbreaking futility some prisoners fully rehabilitated while others, whom the prison officials know full well to be dangerous and unemployable, must be released, *against our judgment,* because a judge far away (who has by this time forgotten all about it) said that five years was enough. In my frequent visits to prisons I am always astonished at how rarely the judges who have prescribed the "treatment" come to see whether or not it is effective. What if doctors who sent their seriously ill patients to hospitals never called to see them!

THE END OF TABOO

As more states adopt diagnostic centers directed toward getting the prisoners *out* of jail and back to work, under modern, well-structured parole systems, the taboo on jail and prison, like that on state hospitals, will begin to diminish. Once it was a lifelong disgrace to have been in either. Lunatics, as they were cruelly called, were feared and avoided. Today only the ignorant retain this phobia. Cancer was then considered a *shameful* thing to have, and victims of it were afraid to mention it, or have it correctly treated, because they did not want to be disgraced. The time will come when offenders, much as we disapprove of their offenses, will no longer be unemployable untouchables.

To a physician discussing the wiser treatment of our fellow men it seems hardly necessary to add that under no circumstances should we kill them. It was never considered right for doctors to kill their patients, no matter how hopeless their condition. True, some patients in state institutions have undoubtedly been executed without benefit of sentence. They were a nuisance, expensive to keep and dangerous to release. Various people took it upon themselves to put an end to the matter, and I have even heard them boast of it. The Hitler regime had the same philosophy.

But in most civilized countries today we have a higher opinion of the rights of the individual and of the limits to the state's power. We know, too, that for the most part the death penalty is inflicted upon obscure, impoverished, defective, and friendless individuals. We know that it intimidates juries in their efforts to determine guilt without prejudice. We know that it is being eliminated in one state after another, most recently Delaware. We know that in practice it has almost disappeared—for over seven thousand capital crimes last year there were less than one hundred executions. But vast sums of money are still being spent—let us say wasted—in legal contests to determine whether or not an individual, even one known to have been mentally ill, is now healthy enough for the state to hang him. (I am informed that such a case has recently cost the State of California $400,000!)

Most of all, we know that no state employees—except perhaps some that ought to be patients themselves—want a job on the killing squad, and few wardens can stomach this piece of medievalism in their own prisons. For example, two officials I know recently quarreled because each wished to have the hanging of a prisoner carried out on the other's premises.

Capital punishment is, in my opinion, morally wrong. It has a bad effect on everyone, especially those involved in it. It gives a false sense of security to the public. It is vastly expensive. Worst of all it beclouds the entire issue of motivation in crime, which is so importantly relevant to the question of what to do for and with the criminal that will be most constructive to society as a whole. Punishing—and even killing—criminals may yield a kind of grim gratification; let us all admit that there are times when we are so shocked at the depredations of an offender that we persuade ourselves that this is a man the Creator didn't intend to create, and that we had better help correct the mistake. But playing God in this way has no conceivable moral or scientific justification.

Let us return in conclusion to the initial question: "Verdict guilty— now what?" My answer is that now we, the designated representatives of the society which has failed to integrate this man, which has failed him in some way, hurt him and been hurt by him, should take over. It is *our* move. And our move must be a constructive one, an intelligent one, a purposeful one—not a primitive, retaliatory, offensive move. We, the agents of society, must move to end the game of tit-for-tat and blow-for-blow in which the offender has foolishly and futilely engaged himself and us. We are not driven, as he is, to wild and impulsive actions. With knowledge comes power, and with power there is no need for the frightened vengeance of the old penology. In its place should go a quiet, dignified, therapeutic program for the rehabilitation of the disorganized one, if possible, the protection of society during his treatment period, and his guided return to useful citizenship, as soon as this can be effected.

Punishment v. Rehabilitation

Richard Wasserstrom

There is a view, held most prominently but by no means exclusively by persons in psychiatry, that we ought never punish persons who break the law and that we ought instead to do something much more like what we do when we treat someone who has a disease. According to this view, what we ought to do to all such persons is to do our best to bring it about that they can and will function in a satisfactory way within society. The functional equivalent to the treatment of a disease is the rehabilitation of an offender, and it is a rehabilitative system, not a punishment system, that we ought to have if we are to respond, even to criminals, in anything like a decent, morally defensible fashion.

Karl Menninger has put the proposal this way:

> If we were to follow scientific methods, the convicted offender would be detained indefinitely pending a decision as to whether and how to reintroduce him successfully into society. All the skill and knowledge of modern behavior science would be used to examine his personality assets, his liabilities and potentialities, the environment from which he came, its effects upon him, and his effects upon it.
>
> Having arrived at some diagnostic grasp of the offender's personality, those in charge can decide whether there is a chance that he can be redirected into a mutually satisfactory adaptation to the world. If so, the most suitable techniques in education, industrial training, group administration, and psychotherapy should be selectively applied. All this may be best done extramurally or intramurally. It may require maximum "security" or only minimum "security." If, in due time, perceptible change occurs, the process should be expedited by finding a suitable spot in society and industry for him, and getting him out of prison control and into civil status (with parole control) as quickly as possible.[1]

From *Philosophy and Social Issues: Five Studies* by Richard Wasserstrom. Copyright © 1980 by University of Notre Dame Press. Reprinted by permission.

It is important at the outset to see that there are two very different arguments which might underlie the claim that the functional equivalent of a system of treatment is desirable and in fact always ought to be preferred to a system of punishment.

The first argument fixes upon the desirability of such a system over one of punishment in virtue of the fact that, because no offenders are responsible for their actions, no offenders are ever justifiably punished. The second argument is directed towards establishing that such a system is better than one of punishment even if some or all offenders are responsible for their actions. A good deal of the confusion present in discussions of the virtues of a system of treatment results from a failure to get clear about these two arguments and to keep the two separate. The first is superficially the more attractive and ultimately the less plausible of the two. Each, though, requires its own explication and analysis.

One way in which the first argument often gets stated is in terms of the sickness of offenders. It is, so the argument begins, surely wrong to punish someone for something that he or she could not help, for something for which he or she was not responsible. No one can help being sick. No one ought, therefore, ever be punished for being sick. As the Supreme Court has observed: "Even one day in prison would be cruel and unusual punishment for the 'crime' of having a common cold."[2] Now, it happens to be the case that everyone who commits a crime is sick. Hence, it is surely wrong to punish anyone who commits a crime. What is more, when a response is appropriate, the appropriate response to sickness is treatment. For this reason what we ought to do is to treat offenders, not punish them.

One difficulty with this argument is that the relevance of sickness to the rightness or wrongness of the punishment of offenders is anything but obvious. Indeed, it appears that the conclusion depends upon a non sequitur just because we seldom, if ever, seek to punish people for being sick. Instead we punish them for actions they perform. On the surface, at least, it would seem that even if someone is sick, and even if the person cannot help being sick, this in no way implies that none of his or her actions could have been other than what it was. Thus, if the argument against ever punishing the guilty criminal is to be at all persuasive, it must be shown that for one reason or another, the sickness which afflicts all criminals must affect their actions in such a way that they are thereby prevented ever from acting differently. Construed in this fashion, the argument is at least coherent and responsive. Unfortunately, there is now no reason to be persuaded by it.

It might be persuasive were there any reason to believe that all criminal acts were, for example, instances of compulsive behavior; if, that is, we thought it likely to be true that all criminals were in some obvious and distinguishable sense afflicted by or subjected to irresistible impulses which compelled them to break the law. For there are people who do seem to be subjected to irresistible impulses and who are thereby unable to keep themselves from, among other things, committing crimes. And it is surely troublesome if not clearly wrong to punish them for these actions. Thus, the kleptomaniac or the person who is truly already addicted to narcotics does seem to be suffering from something resembling a sickness and, moreover, to be suffering from something which makes it very difficult if not impossible for such a person to control the actions so compelled. Pity not blame seems appropriate, as does treatment rather than punishment.[3]

Now, the notion of compulsive behavior is not without difficulties of its own. How strong, for instance, does a compulsion have to be before it cannot be resisted? Would someone be a kleptomaniac only if such an individual would steal an object even though a policeman were known by the person to be present and observing every move? Is there anything more that is meant by compulsive behavior than the fact that it is behavior which is inexplicable or unaccountable in terms of the motives and purposes people generally have? More importantly, perhaps, why do we and why should we suppose that the apparently "motiveless" behavior must be the product of compulsions which are less resistible than those to which we all are at times subjected? As has been observed, ". . . it is by no means self-evident that [a wealthy] person's yearnings for valueless [items] are inevitably stronger or more nearly irresistible than the poor man's hunger for a square meal or for a pack of cigarettes."[4]

But while there are problems such as these, the more basic one is simply that there is no reason to believe that all criminal acts are instances of compulsive behavior. Even if there are persons who are victims of irresistible impulses, and even if we ought always to treat and never to punish such persons, it surely does not follow that everyone who commits a crime is doing a compulsive act. And because this is so, it cannot be claimed that all criminals ought to be exempted from punishment—treated instead—because they have a sickness of this sort.

It might be argued, though, that while compulsive behavior accounts only for some criminal acts, there are other sicknesses which account for the remainder. At this juncture the most ready candidate to absorb the remaining cases is that of insanity. The law, for example, has always been willing to concede that a person ought never be punished if the person was so sick or so constituted that he or she did not know the nature or quality of the act, or if this were known, that the person did not know that the act was wrong. And more recently, attempts have been made, sometimes successfully, to expand this exemption to include any person whose criminal action was substantially the product of mental defect or disease.[5]

Once again, though, the crucial point is not the formulation of the most appropriate test for insanity, but the fact that it is far from evident, even under the most "liberal" test imaginable, that it would be true that everyone who commits a crime would be found to be sick and would be found to have been afflicted with a sickness which in some sense rendered the action in question unavoidable. Given all of our present knowledge, there is simply every reason to suppose that some of the people who do commit crimes are neither subject to irresistible impulses, incapable of knowing what they are doing, nor suffering from some other definite mental disease. And, if this is so, then it is a mistake to suppose that the treatment of criminals is on this ground always to be preferred to their punishment.

There is, though, one final version of the claim that every criminal action is excusable on grounds of the sickness of the actor. And this version does succeed in bringing all the remaining instances of criminality, not otherwise excusable, within the catgeory of sickness. It does so only by making the defining characteristic or symptom of mental illness the commission of an illegal act. All criminals, so this argument goes, who are not insane or subject to irresistible impulses are sociopaths—people afflicted with that mental illness which manifests itself exclusively through the commission of antisocial acts. This sickness, like any other sickness, should be treated rather than punished.

Once this stage of the discussion is reached, it is important to be aware of what has happened. In particular, there is no longer the evidentiary claim that all criminal acts are caused by some sickness. Instead there is the bare assertion that this must be so—an assertion, moreover, of a somewhat deceptive character. The illness which afflicts these criminals *is simply* the criminal behavior itself. The disease which is the reason for not punishing the action is identical with the action itself. At this point any attempt to substantiate or disprove the existence of a relationship between sickness and crime is ruled out of order. The presence of mental illnesses of these kinds cannot, therefore, be reasons for not punishing, or for anything else.

Thus, even if it is true that we ought never to punish and that we ought always to treat someone whose criminal action was unavoidable because the product of some mental or physical disease—even if we concede all this— it has yet to be demonstrated, without begging the question, that all persons who commit crimes are afflicted with some disease or sickness of this kind. And, therefore, if it is always wrong to punish people, or if it is always preferable to treat them, then an argument of a different sort must be forthcoming.

In general form that different argument is this: The legal system ought to abandon its attempts to assess responsibility and punish offenders and it ought instead to focus solely on the question of how most appropriately the legal system can deal with, i.e., rehabilitate if possible, the person presently before the court—not, however, because everyone is sick, but because no good comes from punishing even those who are responsible.

One such proponent of this view is Lady Barbara Wootton.[6] Her position is an ostensibly simple one. What she calls for is the "elimination" of responsibility. The state of mind, or *mens rea*, of the actor at the time he or she committed the act in question is no longer to be determinative—in the way it now is—of how he or she shall be dealt with by society. Rather, she asserts, when someone has been accused of violating the law we ought to have a social mechanism that will ask and answer two distinct questions: Did the accused in fact do the act in question? If he or she did, given all that we know about this person (including his or her state of mind), what is the appropriate form of social response to him or her?

Lady Wootton's proposal is for a system of social control that is thoroughly forward-looking, and in this sense, rehabilitative in perspective. With the elimination of responsibility comes the elimination of the need by the legal system to distinguish any longer between wickedness and disease. And with the eradication of this distinction comes the substitution of a forward-looking, treatment system for the backward-looking, punitive system of criminal law.

The mental state or condition of the offender will continue to be important but in a different way. "Such conditions . . . become relevant, not to the question of determining the measure of culpability but to the choice of the treatment most likely to be effective in discouraging him from offending again. . . ."[7]

> . . . one of the most important consequences must be to obscure the present rigid distinction between the penal and the medical institution. . . . For purposes of convenience offenders for whom medical treatment is indicated will doubtless tend to be allocated to one building, and those for whom medicine has nothing to offer to another; but *the formal distinction between prison and hospital will become blurred, and, one may reasonably expect, eventually obliterated altogether. Both will be simply "places of safety" in which offenders receive the treatment which experience suggests is most likely to evoke the desired response.*[8]

Thus, on this view even if a person was responsible when he or she acted and blameworthy for having so acted, we still ought to behave toward him or her in roughly the same way that we behave toward someone who is sick—we ought, in other words, to do something very much like treating him or her. Why? Because this just makes more sense than punishment. The fact that he or she was responsible is simply not very relevant. It is wrong of course to punish people who are sick; but even with those who are well, the more humane and civilized approach is one that concerns itself solely with the question of how best to effect the most rapid and complete rehabilitation or "cure" of the offender. The argument is not that no one is responsible or blameworthy; instead, it is that these descriptions are simply irrelevant to what, on moral grounds, ought to be the only significant considerations, namely, what mode of behavior toward the offender is most apt to maximize the likelihood that he or she will not in the future commit those obnoxious or dangerous acts that are proscribed by the law. The only goal ought to be rehabilitation (in this extended sense of "rehabilitation"), the only issue how to bring about the rehabilitation of the offender.

The moral good sense of this approach can be perceived most clearly, so the argument goes on, when we contrast this thoroughly forward-looking point of view with punishment. For if there is one thing which serves to differentiate any form of punishment from that of treatment, it is that punishment necessarily permits the possibility and even the desirability that punishment will be imposed upon an offender even though he or she is fully "cured"—even though there is no significant likelihood that he or she will behave improperly in the future. And, in every such case in which a person is punished—in every case in which the infliction of the punishment will help the offender not at all (and may in fact harm him or her immeasurably)—the act of punishment is, on moral grounds, seriously offensive. Even if it were true that some of the people who commit crimes are responsible and blameworthy, and even if it were the case that we had meaningful techniques at our disposal for distinguishing those who are responsible from those who are not—still, every time we inflict a punishment on someone who will not be benefited by it, we commit a seriously immoral act. This claim, or something like it, lies, I think, at the base of the case which can be made against the punishment even of the guilty. For it is true that any system of punishment does require that some people will be made to suffer even though the suffering will help them not at all. It is this which the analogue to a system of treatment, a rehabilitative system such as Lady Wootton's, expressly prevents, and it is in virtue of this that such a system might be thought preferable.[9]

There are, I think, both practical and theoretical objections to a proposal such as this. The practical objections concern, first, the possibility that certain "effective" treatments may themselves be morally objectionable, and, second, the possibility that this way of viewing offenders may create a world in which we all become indifferent to the characteristics that distinguish those who are responsible from those who are not. The ease, for example, with which someone like Menninger tends to see the criminal not as an adult but as a "grown-up child"[10] says something about the ease with which a kind of paternalistic manipulativeness could readily pervade a system composed of "places of safety."[11]

These are, though, contingent rather than necessary worries. A system organized in accordance with this rehabilitative ideal could have a view that certain therapies were impermissible on moral grounds, just as it could also treat all of the persons involved with all of the respect they deserved as persons. Indeed, it is important when comparing and contrasting proposals for rehabilitative systems with punishment to make certain that the comparisons are of things that are comparable. There are abuses present in most if not all institutional therapeutic systems in existence today, but there are also abuses present in most if not all institutional penal systems in existence today. And the practical likelihood of the different abuses is certainly worth taking seriously in trying to evaluate the alternatives. What is not appropriate, however, is to contrast either an ideal of the sort proposed by Wootton or Menninger with an existing penal one, or an ideal, just penal system with an existing therapeutic one.[12]

These matters to one side, one of the chief theoretical objections to a proposal of the sort just described is that it ignores the whole question of general deterrence. Were we to have a system such as that envisioned by Lady Wootton or Menninger, we would ask one and only one question of each person who violated the law: What is the best, most efficacious thing to do to this individual to diminish substantially the likelihood that he or she will misbehave in this, or similar fashion, again? If there is nothing at all that need be done in order for us to be quite confident that he or she will not misbehave again (perhaps because the person is extremely contrite, or because we are convinced it was an impulsive, or otherwise unlikely-to-be-repeated act), then the logic of this system requires that the individual be released forthwith. For in this system it is the future conduct of the actor, and it alone, that is the only relevant consideration. There is simply no room within this way of thinking to take into account the achievement of general deterrence. H. L. A. Hart has put the matter this way in explaining why the *reform* (when any might be called for) of the prisoner cannot be the general justifying aim of a system of punishment.

> The objection of assigning to Reform this place in punishment is not merely that punishment entails suffering and reform does not; but that Reform is essentially a remedial step for which ex hypothesi there is an opportunity only at the point where the criminal law has failed in its primary task of securing society from the evil which breach of the law involves. Society is divisible at any moment into two classes (i) those who have actually broken a given law and (ii) those who have not yet broken it but may. *To take Reform as the dominant objective would be to forego the hope of influencing the second—and in relation to the more serious offenses—numerically much greater class. We should thus subordinate the prevention of first offenses to the prevention of recidivism.*[13]

A system of punishment will on this view find its justification in the fact that the announcement of penalties and their infliction upon those who break the laws induces others to obey the laws. The question why punish anyone at all *is* answered by Hart. We punish because we thereby deter potential offenders from becoming actual offenders. For Hart, the case for punishment as a general social practice or institution rests on the prevention of crime; it is not to be found either in the inherent appropriateness of punishing offenders or in the contingently "corrective" or rehabilitative powers of fines or imprisonments on some criminals.

Yet, despite appearances, the appeal to general deterrence is not as different as might be supposed from the appeal to a rehabilitative ideal. In both cases, the justification for doing something (or nothing) to the offender rests upon the good consequences that will ensue. General deterrence just as much as rehabilitation views what should be done to offenders as a question of *social control.* It is a way of inducing those who can control their behavior to regulate it in such a way that it will conform to the dictates of the law. The disagreement with those who focus upon rehabilitation is only over the question of whose behavioral modification justifies the imposition of deprivations upon the criminals. Proponents of general deterrence say it is the modification of the behavior of the noncriminals that matters; proponents of rehabilitation say it is the modification of the behavior of the criminals that is decisive. Thus, a view such as Hart's is less a justification of punishment than of a system of threats of punishment. For if the rest of society could be convinced that offenders would be made to undergo deprivations that persons would not wish to undergo we would accomplish all that the deterrent theory would have us achieve through our somewhat more visible applications of these deprivations to offenders. This is so because it is the belief that punishment will follow the commission of an offense that deters potential offenders. The actual punishment of persons is on this view necessary in order to keep the threat of punishment credible. . . .

NOTES

1. Menninger, "Therapy, Not Punishment," reprinted in Murphy (ed.), *Punishment and Rehabilitation* (Belmont, California: Wadsworth Publishing Co., 1973), p. 136. [See pages 47-55 of the present volume.]

2. Robinson v. California, 370 U.S. 660 (1962).

3. The Supreme Court has worried about this problem in, for example, the case of chronic alcoholism, in Powell v. Texas, 392 U.S. 514 (1968). The discussion in this and related cases is neither very clear nor very illuminating.

4. Barbara Wootton, *Social Science and Social Pathology* (London: G. Allen & Unwin, 1959), p. 235.

5. See, e.g., Durham v. United States, 214 F. 2d 862 (D.C. Cir., 1954); United States v. Brawner, 471 F. 2d 969 (D.C. Cir., 1972); and Model Penal Code § 4.01.

6. Barbara Wootton, *Crime and the Criminal Law* (London: Stevens, 1963).

7. Ibid., p. 77.

8. Ibid., pp. 79-80 (emphasis added).

9. There are some additional, more practical arguments that might be offered in support of such a proposal.

To begin with, by making irrelevant the question of whether the actor was responsible when he or she acted, the operation of the criminal law could be greatly simplified. More specifically, by "eliminating" the issue of responsibility we thereby necessarily eliminate the requirement that the law continue to attempt to make those terribly difficult judgments of legal responsibility which our system of punishment requires to be made. And, as a practical matter, at least, this is no small consideration. For surely there is no area in which the techniques of legal adjudication have functioned less satisfactorily than in that of determining the actor's legal responsibility as of the time he violated the law. The attempts to formulate and articulate satisfactory and meaningful criteria of responsibility; the struggles to develop and then isolate specialists who can meaningfully and impartially relate these criteria to the relevant medical concepts and evidence; and the difficulties encountered in requiring the traditional legal fact-finding mechanism—the jury— ultimately to resolve these issues—all of these bear impressive witness, it could plausibly be claimed, for the case for ceasing to make the effort.

In addition, it is no doubt fair to say that most people do not like to punish others. They may, indeed, have no objection to the punishment of others; but the actual task of inflicting and overseeing the infliction of an organized set of punishments is distasteful to most. It is all too easy, therefore, and all too typical, for society to entrust the administration of punishments to those who, if they do not actually enjoy it, at least do not find it unpleasant. Just as there is no necessary reason for punishments ever to be needlessly severe, so there is no necessary reason for those who are charged with the duty of punishing to be brutal or unkind. Nonetheless, it is simply a fact that it is difficult, if not impossible, to attract sensitive, kindly or compassionate persons to assume this charge. No such analogous problem, it might be argued, attends the call for treatment.

10. "What might deter the reader from conduct which his neighbors would not like does not necessarily deter the grown-up child of vastly different background. . . .

"It is not the successful criminal upon whom we inflict our antiquated penal system. It is the unsuccessful criminal, the criminal who really doesn't know how to commit crimes and who gets caught. . . . The clumsy, the desperate, the obscure, the friendless, the defective, the diseased—these men who commit crimes that do not come off— are bad actors, indeed. But they are not the professional criminals, many of whom occupy high places." Menninger, op. cit., supra note 12, pp. 134-35.

11. These are discussed persuasively and in detail by Morris in his important article, "Persons and Punishment," 52 *The Monist* 475 (1968), pp. 476-90.

12. I think that Morris at times indulges in an improper comparison of the two. Ibid.

13. H. L. A. Hart, *The Concept of Law* (Oxford: At the Clarendon Press, 1961), p. 181 (emphasis added).

Persons and Punishment

Herbert Morris

"They acted and looked . . . at us, and around in our house, in a way that had about it the feeling—at least for me—that we were not people. In their eyesight we were just things, that was all."

Malcolm X

"We have no right to treat a man like a dog."

Governor Maddox of Georgia

Alfredo Traps in Durrenmatt's tale discovers that he has brought off, all by himself, a murder involving considerable ingenuity. The mock prosecutor in the tale demands the death penalty "as reward for a crime that merits admiration, astonishment, and respect." Traps is deeply moved; indeed, he is exhilarated, and the whole of his life becomes more heroic, and, ironically, more precious. His defense attorney proceeds to argue that Traps was not only innocent but incapable of guilt, "a victim of the age." This defense Traps disavows with indignation and anger. He makes claim to the murder as his and demands the prescribed punishment—death.

The themes to be found in this macabre tale do not often find their way into philosophical discussions of punishment. These discussions deal with large and significant questions of whether or not we ever have the right to punish, and if we do, under what conditions, to what degree, and in what manner. There is a tradition, of course, not notable for its present vitality, that is closely linked with motifs in Durrenmatt's tale of crime and punishment. Its adherents have urged that justice requires a person be punished if he is guilty. Sometimes—though rarely—these philosophers have expressed themselves in terms of the criminal's *right to be punished*. Reaction to the claim that there is such a right has been

Reprinted, with changes, from *Monist* 52 (October 1968): 475-494, by permission of the publisher.

astonishment combined, perhaps, with a touch of contempt for the perversity of the suggestion. A strange right that no one would ever wish to claim! With that flourish the subject is buried and the right disposed of. In this paper the subject is resurrected.

My aim is to argue for four propositions concerning rights that will certainly strike some as not only false but preposterous: first . . . that we have a right to punishment [and] that this right derives from a fundamental human right to be treated as a person. . . .

1. When someone claims that there is a right to be free, we can easily imagine situations in which the right is infringed and easily imagine situations in which there is a point to asserting or claiming the right. With the right to be punished, matters are otherwise. The immediate reaction to the claim that there is such a right is puzzlement. And the reasons for this are apparent. People do not normally value pain and suffering. Punishment is associated with pain and suffering. When we think about punishment we naturally think of the strong desire most persons have to avoid it, to accept, for example, acquittal of a criminal charge with relief and eagerly, if convicted, to hope for pardon or probation. Adding, of course, to the paradoxical character of the claim of such a right is difficulty in imagining circumstances in which it would be denied one. When would one rightly demand punishment and meet with any threat of the claim being denied?

So our first task is to see when the claim of such a right would have a point. I want to approach this task by setting out two complex types of institutions both of which are designed to maintain some degree of social control. In the one a central concept is punishment for wrongdoing and in the other the central concepts are control of dangerous individuals and treatment of disease.

Let us first turn attention to the institutions in which punishment is involved. The institutions I describe will resemble those we ordinarily think of as institutions of punishment; they will have, however, additional features we associate with a system of just punishment.

Let us suppose that men are constituted roughly as they now are, with a rough equivalence in strength and abilities, a capacity to be injured by each other and to make judgments that such injury is undesirable, a limited strength of will, and a capacity to reason and to conform conduct to rules. Applying to the conduct of these men are a group of rules, ones I shall label 'primary', which closely resemble the core rules of our criminal law, rules that prohibit violence and deception and compliance with which provides benefits for all persons. These benefits consist in noninterference by others with what each person values, such matters as continuance of life and bodily security. The rules define a sphere for each person, then, which is immune from interference by others. Making possible this mutual benefit is the assumption by individuals of a burden. The burden consists in the exercise of self-restraint by individuals over inclinations that would, if satisfied, directly interfere or create a substantial risk of interference with others in proscribed ways. If a person fails to exercise self-restraint even though he might have and gives in to such inclinations, he renounces a burden which others have voluntarily assumed and thus gains an advantage which others, who have restrained themselves, do not possess. This system, then, is one in which the rules establish a mutuality of benefit and burden and in which the benefits of noninterference are conditional upon the assumption of burdens.

Connecting punishment with the violation of these primary rules, and making public the provision for punishment, is both reasonable and just. First, it is only reasonable that those who voluntarily comply with the rules be provided some assurance that they will not be assuming burdens which others are unprepared to assume. Their disposition to comply voluntarily will diminish as they learn that others are with impunity renouncing burdens they are assuming. Second, fairness dictates that a system in which benefits and burdens are equally distributed have a mechanism designed to prevent a maldistribution in the benefits and burdens. Thus, sanctions are attached to noncompliance with the primary rules so as to induce compliance with the primary rules among those who may be disinclined to obey. In this way the likelihood of an unfair distribution is diminished.

Third, it is just to punish those who have violated the rules and caused the unfair distribution of benefits and burdens. A person who violates the rules has something others have—the benefits of the system—but by renouncing what others have assumed, the burdens of self-restraint, he has acquired an unfair advantage. Matters are not even until this advantage is in some way erased. Another way of putting it is that he owes something to others, for he has something that does not rightfully belong to him. Justice—that is punishing such individuals—restores the equilibrium of benefits and burdens by taking from the individual what he owes, that is, exacting the debt. It is important to see that the equilibrium may be restored in another way. Forgiveness—with its legal analogue of a pardon—while not the righting of an unfair distribution by making one pay his debt is, nevertheless, a restoring of the equilibrium by forgiving the debt. Forgiveness may be viewed, at least in some types of cases, as a gift after the fact, erasing a debt, which had the gift been given before the fact, would not have created a debt. But the practice of pardoning has to proceed sensitively, for it may endanger in a way the practice of justice does not, the maintenance of an equilibrium of benefits and burdens. If all are indiscriminately pardoned less incentive is provided individuals to restrain their inclinations, thus increasing the incidence of persons taking what they do not deserve.

There are also in this system we are considering a variety of operative principles compliance with which provides some guarantee that the system of punishment does not itself promote an unfair distribution of benefits and burdens. For one thing, provision is made for a variety of defenses, each one of which can be said to have as its object diminishing the chances of forcibly depriving a person of benefits others have if that person has not derived an unfair advantage. A person has not derived an unfair advantage if he could not have restrained himself or if it is unreasonable to expect him to behave otherwise than he did. Sometimes the rules preclude punishment of classes of persons such as children. Sometimes they provide a defense if on a particular occasion a person lacked the capacity to conform his conduct to the rules. Thus, someone who in an epileptic seizure strikes another is excused. Punishment in these cases would be punishment of the innocent, punishment of those who do not voluntarily renounce a burden others have assumed. Punishment in such cases, then, would not equalize but rather cause an unfair distribution in benefits and burdens.

Along with principles providing defenses there are requirements that the rules be prospective and relatively clear so that persons have a fair opportunity to comply with the rules. There are, also, rules governing, among other matters, the burden of proof, who shall bear it and what it shall be, the prohibition on double jeopardy, and the privilege against self-incrimination. Justice requires conviction of the guilty, and requires their punishment, but in setting out to fulfill the demands of justice we may, of course, because we are not omniscient, cause injustice by convicting and punishing the innocent. The resolution arrived at in the system I am describing consists in weighing as the greater evil the punishment of the innocent. The primary function of the system of rules was to provide individuals with a sphere of interest immune from interference. Given this goal, it is determined to be a greater evil for society to interfere unjustifiably with an individual by depriving him of good than for the society to fail to punish those that have unjustifiably interfered.

Finally, because the primary rules are designed to benefit all and because the punishments prescribed for their violation are publicized and the defenses respected, there is some plausibility in the exaggerated claim that in choosing to do an act violative of the rules an individual has chosen to be punished. This way of putting matters brings to our attention the extent to which, when the system is as I have described it, the criminal "has brought the punishment upon himself" in contrast to those cases where it would be misleading to say "he has brought it upon himself," cases, for example, where one does not know the rules or is punished in the absence of fault.

To summarize, then: first, there is a group of rules guiding the behavior of individuals in the community which establish spheres of interest immune from interference by others; second, provision is made for what is generally regarded as a deprivation of some thing of value if the rules are violated; third, the deprivations visited upon any person are justified by that person's having violated the rules; fourth, the deprivation, in this just system of punishment, is linked to rules that fairly distribute benefits and burdens and to procedures that strike some balance between not punishing the guilty and punishing the innocent, a class defined as those who have not voluntarily done acts violative of the law, in which it is evident that the evil of punishing the innocent is regarded as greater than the nonpunishment of the guilty.

At the core of many actual legal systems one finds, of course, rules and procedures of the kind I have sketched. It is obvious, though, that any ongoing legal system differs in significant respects from what I have presented here, containing 'pockets of injustice'.

I want now to sketch an extreme version of a set of institutions of a fundamentally different kind, institutions proceeding on a conception of man which appears to be basically at odds with that operative within a system of punishment.

Rules are promulgated in this system that prohibit certain types of injuries and harms.

In this world we are now to imagine when an individual harms another his conduct is to be regarded as a symptom of some pathological condition in the way a running nose is a symptom of a cold. Actions diverging from some conception of the normal are viewed as manifestations of a disease in the way in which we might today regard the arm and leg movements of an epileptic during a seizure. Actions conforming to what is normal are assimilated to the normal and healthy functioning of bodily organs. What a person does, then, is assimilated, on this conception, to what we believe today, or at least most of us believe today, a person undergoes. We draw a distinction between the operation of the kidney and raising an arm on request. This distinction between mere events or happenings and human actions is erased in our imagined system.[1]

There is, however, bound to be something strange in this erasing of a recognized distinction, for, as with metaphysical suggestions generally, and I take this to be one, the distinction may be reintroduced but given a different description, for example, 'happenings with X type of causes' and 'happenings with Y type of causes'. Responses of different kinds, today legitimated by our distinction between happenings and actions, may be legitimated by this new manner of description. And so there may be isomorphism between a system recognizing the distinction and one erasing it. Still, when this distinction is erased certain tendencies of thought and responses might naturally arise that would tend to affect unfavorably values respected by a system of punishment.

Let us elaborate on this assimilation of conduct of a certain kind to symptoms of a disease. First, there is something abnormal in both the case of conduct, such as killing another, and a symptom of a disease such as an irregular heart beat. Second, there are causes for this abnormality in action such that once we know of them we can explain the abnormality as we now can explain the symptoms of many physical diseases. The abnormality is looked upon as a happening with a causal explanation rather than an action for which there were reasons. Third, the causes that account for the abnormality interfere with the normal functioning of the body, or, in the case of killing with what is regarded as a normal functioning of an individual. Fourth, the abnormality is in some way a part of the individual, necessarily involving his body. A well going dry might satisfy our three foregoing conditions of disease symptoms, but it is hardly a disease or the symptom of one. Finally, and most obscure, the abnormality arises in some way from within the individual. If Jones is hit with a mallet by Smith, Jones may reel about and fall on James who may be injured. But this abnormal conduct of Jones is not regarded as a symptom of disease. Smith, not Jones, is suffering from some pathological condition.

With this view of man the institutions of social control respond, not with punishment, but with either preventive detention, in case of 'carriers', or therapy in the case of those manifesting pathological symptoms. The logic of sickness implies the logic of therapy. And therapy and punishment differ widely in their implications. In bringing out some of these differences I want again to draw attention to the important fact that while the distinctions we now draw are erased in the therapy world, they may, in fact, be reintroduced but under different descriptions. To the extent they are, we really have a punishment system combined with a therapy system. I am concerned now, however, with what the implications would be were the world indeed one of therapy and not a disguised world of punishment and therapy, for I want to suggest tendencies of thought that arise when one is immersed in the ideology of disease and therapy.

First, punishment is the imposition upon a person who is believed to be at fault of something commonly believed to be a deprivation where that deprivation is justified by the person's guilty behavior. It is associated with resentment, for the guilty are those who have done what they have no right to do by failing to exercise restraint when they might have and where others have. Therapy is not a response to a person who is at fault. We respond to an individual, not because of what he has done, but because of some condition from which he is suffering. If he is no longer suffering from the condition, treatment no longer has a point. Punishment, then, focuses on the past; therapy on the present. Therapy is normally associated with compassion for what one undergoes, not resentment for what one has illegitimately done.

Second, with therapy, unlike punishment, we do not seek to deprive the person of something acknowledged as a good, but seek rather to help and to benefit the individual who is suffering by ministering to his illness in the hope that the person can be cured. The good we attempt to do is not a reward for desert. The individual suffering has not merited by his disease the good we seek to bestow upon him but has, because he is a creature that has the capacity to feel pain, a claim upon our sympathies and help.

Third, we saw with punishment that its justification was related to maintaining and restoring a fair distribution of benefits and burdens. Infliction of the prescribed punishment carries the implication, then, that one has 'paid one's debt' to society, for the punishment is the taking from the person of something commonly recognized as valuable. It is this conception of 'a debt owed' that may permit, as I suggested earlier, under certain conditions, the nonpunishment of the guilty, for operative within a system of punishment may be a concept analogous to forgiveness, namely pardoning. Who it is that we may pardon and under what conditions—contrition with its elements of self-punishment no doubt plays a role—I shall not go into though it is clearly a matter of the greatest practical and theoretical interest. What is clear is that the conceptions of 'paying a debt' or 'having a debt forgiven' or pardoning have no place in a system of therapy.

Fourth, with punishment there is an attempt at some equivalence between the advantage gained by the wrongdoer—partly based upon the seriousness of the interest invaded, partly on the state of mind with which the wrongful act was performed—and the punishment meted out. Thus, we can understand a prohibition on 'cruel and unusual punishments' so that disproportionate pain and suffering are avoided. With therapy attempts at proportionality make no sense. It is perfectly plausible giving someone who kills a pill and treating for a lifetime within an institution one who has broken a dish and manifested accident proneness. We have the concept of 'painful treatment'. We do not have the concept of 'cruel treatment'. Because treatment is regarded as a benefit, though it may involve pain, it is natural that less restraint is exercised in bestowing it, than in inflicting punishment. Further, protests with respect to treatment are likely to be assimilated to the complaints of one whose leg must be amputated in order for him to live, and, thus, largely disregarded. To be sure, there is operative in the therapy world some conception of the "cure being worse than the disease," but if the disease is manifested in conduct harmful to others, and if being a normal operating human being is valued highly, there will naturally be considerable pressure to find the cure acceptable.

Fifth, the rules in our system of punishment governing conduct of individuals were rules violation of which involved either direct interference with others or the creation of a substantial risk of such interference. One could imagine adding to this system of primary rules other rules proscribing preparation to do acts violative of the primary rules and even rules proscribing thoughts. Objection to such suggestions would have many sources but a principal one would consist in its involving the infliction of punishment on too great a number of persons who would not, because of a change of mind, have violated the primary rules. Though we are interested in diminishing violations of the primary rules, we are not prepared to punish too many individuals who would never have violated the rules in order to achieve this aim. In a system motivated solely by a preventive and curative ideology there would be less reason to wait until symptoms manifest themselves in socially harmful conduct. It is understandable that we should wish at the earliest possible stage to arrest the development of the disease. In the punishment system, because we are dealing with deprivations, it is understandable that we should forbear from imposing them until we are quite sure of guilt. In the therapy system, dealing as it does with benefits, there is less reason for forbearance from treatment at an early stage.

Sixth, a variety of procedural safeguards we associate with punishment have less significance in a therapy system. To the degree objections to double jeopardy and self-incrimination are based on a wish to decrease the chances of the innocent being convicted and punished, a therapy system, unconcerned with this problem, would disregard such safeguards. When one is out to help people there is also little sense in urging that the burden of proof be on those providing the help. And there is less point to imposing the burden of proving that the conduct was pathological beyond a reasonable doubt. Further, a jury system which, within a system of justice, serves to make accommodations to the individual situation and to introduce a human element, would play no role or a minor one in a world where expertise is required in making determinations of disease and treatment.

In our system of punishment an attempt was made to maximize each individual's freedom of choice by first of all delimiting by rules certain spheres of conduct immune from interference by others. The punishment associated with these primary rules paid deference to an individual's free choice by connecting punishment to a freely chosen act violative of the rules, thus giving some plausibility to the claim, as we saw, that what a person received by way of punishment he himself had chosen. With the world of disease and therapy all this changes and the individual's free choice ceases to be a determinative factor in how others respond to him. All those principles of our own legal system that minimize the chances of punishment of those who have not chosen to do acts violative of the rules tend to lose their point in the therapy system, for how we respond in a therapy system to a person is not conditioned upon what he has chosen but rather on what symptoms he has manifested or may manifest and what the best therapy for the disease is that is suggested by the symptoms.

Now, it is clear I think, that were we confronted with the alternatives I have sketched, between a system of just punishment and a thoroughgoing system of treatment, a system, that is, that did not reintroduce concepts appropriate to punishment, we could see the point in claiming that a person has a right to be punished, meaning by this that a person had a right to all those institutions and practices linked to punishment. For these would provide him with, among other things, a far greater ability to predict what would happen to him on the occurrence of certain events than the therapy system. There is the inestimable value to each of us of having the responses of others to us determined over a wide range of our lives by what we choose rather than what they choose. A person has a right to institutions that respect his choices. Our punishment system does; our therapy system does not.

Apart from those aspects of our therapy model which would relate to serious limitations on personal liberty, there are clearly objections of a more profound kind to the mode of thinking I have associated with the therapy model.

First, human beings pride themselves in having capacities that animals do not. A common way, for example, of arousing shame in a child is to compare the child's conduct to that of an animal. In a system where all actions are assimilated to happenings we are assimilated to creatures—indeed, it is more extreme than this—whom we have always thought possessed of less than we. Fundamental to our practice of praise and order of attainment is that one who can do more—one who is capable of more and one who does more—is more worthy of respect and admiration. And we have thought of ourselves as capable where animals are not of making, of creating, among other things, ourselves. The conception of man I have outlined would provide us with a status that today, when our conduct is assimilated to it in moral criticism, we consider properly evocative of shame.

Second, if all human conduct is viewed as something men undergo, thrown into question would be the appropriateness of that extensive range of peculiarly human satisfactions that derive from a sense of achievement. For these satisfactions we shall have to substitute those mild satisfactions attendant upon a healthy well-functioning body. Contentment is our lot if we are fortunate; intense satisfaction at achievement is entirely inappropriate.

Third, in the therapy world nothing is earned and what we receive comes to us through compassion, or through a desire to control us. Resentment is out of place. We can take credit for nothing but must always regard ourselves—if there are selves left to regard once actions disappear—as fortunate recipients of benefits or unfortunate carriers of disease who must be controlled. We know that within our own world human beings who have been so regarded and who come to accept this view of themselves come to look upon themselves as worthless. When what we do is met with resentment, we are indirectly paid something of a compliment.

Fourth, attention should also be drawn to a peculiar evil that may be attendant upon regarding a man's actions as symptoms of disease. The logic of cure will push us toward forms of therapy that inevitably involve changes in the person made against his will. The evil in this would be most apparent in those cases where the agent, whose action is determined to be a manifestation of some disease, does not regard his action in this way. He believes that what he has done is, in fact, 'right' but conception of 'normality' is not the therapeutically accepted one. When we treat an illness we normally treat a condition that the person is not responsible for. He is 'suffering' from some disease and we treat the condition, relieving the person of something preventing his normal functioning. When we begin treating persons for actions that have been chosen, we do not lift from the person something that is interfering with his normal functioning but we change the person so that he functions in a way regarded as normal by the current therapeutic community. We have to change him and his judgments of value. In doing this we display a lack of respect for the moral status of individuals, that is, a lack of respect for the reasoning and choices of individuals. They are but animals who must be conditioned. I think we can understand and, indeed, sympathize with a man's preferring death to being forcibly turned into what he is not.

Finally, perhaps most frightening of all would be the derogation in status of all protests to treatment. If someone believes that he has done something right, and if he protests being treated and changed, the protest will itself be regarded as a sign of some pathological condition, for who would not wish to be cured of an affliction? What this leads to are questions of an important kind about the effect of this conception of man upon what we now understand by reasoning. Here what a person takes to be a reasoned defense of an act is treated, as the action was, on the model of a happening of a pathological kind. Not just a person's acts are taken from him but also his attempt at a reasoned justification for the acts. In a system of punishment a person who has committed a crime may argue that what he did was right. We make him pay the price and we respect his right to retain the judgment he has made. A conception of pathology precludes this form of respect.

It might be objected to the foregoing that all I have shown—if that—is that if the only alternatives open to us are a *just* system of punishment or the mad world of being treated like sick or healthy animals, we do in fact have a right to a system of punishment of this kind. But this hardly shows that we have a right *simpliciter* to punishment as we do, say, to be free. Indeed, it does not even show a right to a just system of punishment, for surely we can, without too much difficulty, imagine situations in which the alternatives to punishment are not this mad world but a world in which we are still treated as persons and there is, for example, not the pain and suffering attendant upon punishment. One such world is one in which there are rules but response to their violation is not the deprivation of some good but forgiveness. Still another type of world would be one in which violation of the rules were responded to by merely comparing the conduct of the person to something commonly regarded as low or filthy, and thus, producing by this mode of moral criticism, feelings of shame rather than feelings of guilt.

I am prepared to allow that these objections have a point. While granting force to the above objections I want to offer a few additional comments with respect to each of them. First, any existent legal system permits the punishment of individuals under circumstances where the conditions I have set forth for a just system have not been satisfied. A glaring example of this would be criminal strict liability which is to be found in our own legal system. Nevertheless, I think it would be difficult to present any system we should regard as a system of punishment that would not still have a great advantage over our imagined therapy system. The system of punishment we imagine may more and more approximate a system of sheer terror in which human beings are treated as animals to be intimidated and prodded. To the degree that the system is of this character it is, in my judgment, not simply an unjust system but one that diverges from what we normally understand by a system of punishment. At least some deference to the choice of individuals is built into the idea of punishment. So there would be some truth in saying we have a right to any system of punishment if the only alternative to it was therapy.

Second, people may imagine systems in which there are rules and in which the response to their violation is not punishment but pardoning, the legal analogue of forgiveness. Surely this is a system to which we would claim a right as against one in which we are made to suffer for violating the rules. There are several comments that need to be made about this. It may be, of course, that a high incidence of pardoning would increase the incidence of rule violations. Further, the difficulty with suggesting pardoning as a general response is that pardoning presupposes the very responses that it is suggested it supplant. A system of deprivations, or a practice of deprivations on the happening of certain actions, underlies the practice of pardoning and forgiving, for it is only where we possess the idea of a wrong to be made up or of a debt owed to others, ideas we acquire within a world in which there have been deprivations for wrong acts, that we have the idea of pardoning for the wrong or forgiving the debt.

Finally, if we look at the responses I suggested would give rise to feelings of shame, we may rightly be troubled with the appropriateness of this response in any community in which each person assumes burdens so that each may derive benefits. In such situations might it not be that individuals have a right to a system of punishment so that each person could be assured that inequities in the distribution of benefits and burdens are unlikely to occur and if they do, procedures exist for correcting them? Further, it may well be that, everything considered, we should prefer the pain and suffering of a system of punishment to a world in which we only experience shame on the doing of wrong acts, for with guilt there are relatively simple ways of ridding ourselves of the feeling we have, that is, gaining forgiveness or taking the punishment, but with shame we have to bear it until we no longer are the person who has behaved in the shameful way. Thus, I suggest that we have, wherever there is a distribution of benefits and burdens of the kind I have described, a right to a system of punishment.

I want also to make clear in concluding this section that I have argued, though very indirectly, not just for a right to a system of punishment, but for a right to be punished once there is in existence such a system. Thus, a man has the right to be punished rather than treated if he is guilty of some offense. And, indeed, one can imagine a case in which, even in the face of an offer of a pardon, a man claims and ought to have acknowledged his right to be punished.

2. The primary reason for preferring the system of punishment as against the system of therapy might have been expressed in terms of the one system treating one as a person and the other not. In invoking the right to be punished, one justifies one's claim by reference to a more fundamental right. I want now to turn attention to this fundamental right and attempt to shed light—it will have to be little, for the topic is immense—on what is meant by 'treating an individual as a person'.

When we talk of not treating a human being as a person or 'showing no respect for one as a person' what we imply by our words is a contrast between the manner in which one acceptably responds to human beings and the manner in which one acceptably responds to animals and inanimate objects. When we treat a human being merely as an animal or some inanimate object our responses to the human being are determined, not by his choices, but ours in disregard of or with indifference to his. And when we 'look upon' a person as less than a person or not a person, we consider the person as incapable of rational choice. In cases of not treating a human being as a person we interfere with a person in such a way that what is done, even if the person is involved in the doing, is done not by the person but by the user of the person. In extreme cases there may even be an elision of a causal chain so that we might say that *X* killed *Z* even though *Y*s hand was the hand that held the weapon, for *Y*s hand may have been entirely in *X*s control. The one agent is in some way treating the other as a mere link in a causal chain. There is, of course, a wide range of cases in which a person is used to accomplish the aim of another and in which the person used is less than fully free. A person may be grabbed against his will and used as a shield. A person may be drugged or hypnotized and then employed for certain ends. A person may be deceived into doing other than he intends doing. A person may be ordered to do something and threatened with harm if he does not and coerced into doing what he does not want to. There is still another range of cases in which individuals are not used, but in which decisions by others are made that affect them in circumstances where they have the capacity for choice and where they are not being treated as persons.

But it is particularly important to look at coercion, for I have claimed that a just system of punishment treats human beings as persons; and it is not immediately apparent how ordering someone to do something and threatening harm differs essentially from having rules supported by threats of harm in case of noncompliance.

There are affinities between coercion and other cases of not treating someone as a person, for it is not the coerced person's choices but the coercer's that are responsible for what is done. But unlike other indisputable cases of not treating one as a person, for example using someone as a shield, there is some choice involved in coercion. And if this is so, why does the coercer stand in any different relation to the coerced person than the criminal law stands to individuals in society?

Suppose the person who is threatened disregards the order and gets the threatened harm. Now suppose he is told, "Well, you did after all bring it upon yourself." There is clearly something strange in this. It is the person doing the threatening and not the person threatened who is responsible. But our reaction to punishment, at least in a system that resembles the one I have described, is precisely that the person violating the rules brought it upon himself. What lies behind these different reactions?

There exist situations in the law, of course, which resemble coercion situations. There are occasions when in the law a person might justifiably say "I am not being treated as a person but being used" and where he might properly react to the punishment as something "he was hardly responsible for." But it is possible to have a system in which it would be misleading to say, over a wide range of cases of punishment for noncompliance, that we are using persons. The clearest case in which it would be inappropriate to so regard punishment would be one in which there were explicit agreement in advance that punishment should follow on the voluntary doing of certain acts. Even if one does not have such conditions satisfied, and obviously such explicit agreements are not characteristic, one can see significant differences between our system of just punishment and a coercion situation.

First, unlike the case with one person coercing another 'to do his will', the rules in our system apply to all, with the benefits and burdens equally distributed. About such a system it cannot be said that some are being subordinated to others or are being used by others or gotten to do things by others. To the extent that the rules are thought to be to the advantage of only some or to the extent there is a maldistribution of benefits and burdens, the difference between coercion and law disappears.

Second, it might be argued that at least any person inclined to act in a manner violative of the rules stands to all others as the person coerced stands to his coercer, and that he, at least, is a person disadvantaged as others are not. It is important here, I think, that he is part of a system in which it is commonly agreed that forbearance from the acts proscribed by the rules provides advantages for all. This system is the accepted setting; it is the norm. Thus, in any coercive situation, it is the coercer who deviates from the norm, with the responsibility of the person he is attempting to coerce, defeated. In a just punishment situation, it is the person deviating from the norm, indeed he might be a coercer, who is responsible, for it is the norm to restrain oneself from acts of that kind. A voluntary agent diverging in his conduct from what is expected or what the norm is, on general causal principles, is regarded as the cause of what results from his conduct.

There is, then, some plausibility in the claim that, in a system of punishment of the kind I have sketched, a person chooses the punishment that is meted out to him. If, then, we can say in such a system that the rules provide none with advantages that others do not have, and further, that what happens to a person is conditioned by that person's choice and not that of others, then we can say that it is a system responding to one as a person.

We treat a human being as a person provided: first, we permit the person to make the choices that will determine what happens to him and second, when our responses to the person are responses respecting the person's choices. When we respond to a person's illness by treating the illness it is neither a case of treating or not treating the individual as a person. When we give a person a gift we are neither treating him or not treating him as a person, unless, of course, he does not wish it, chooses not to have it, but we compel him to accept it.

3. This right to be treated as a person is a fundamental human right belonging to all human beings by virtue of their being human. . . .

If the right is one that we possess by virtue of being human beings, we are immediately confronted with an apparent dilemma. If, to treat another as a person requires that we provide him with reasons for acting and avoid force or deception, how can we justify the force and deception we exercise with respect to children and the mentally ill? If they, too, have a right to be treated as persons are we not constantly infringing their rights? One way out of this is simply to restrict the right to those who satisfy the conditions of being a person. Infants and the insane, it might be argued, do not meet these conditions, and they would not then have the right. Another approach would be to describe the right they possess as a prima facie right to be treated as a person. This right might then be outweighed by other considerations. This approach generally seems to me, as I shall later argue, inadequate.

I prefer this tack. Children possess the right to be treated as persons but they possess this right as an individual might be said in the law of property to possess a future interest. There are advantages in talking of individuals as having a right though complete enjoyment of it is postponed. Brought to our attention, if we ascribe to them the right, is the legitimacy of their complaint if they are not provided with opportunities and conditions assuring their full enjoyment of the right when they acquire the characteristics of persons. More than this, all persons are charged with the sensitive task of not denying them the right to be a person and to be treated as a person by failing to provide the conditions for their becoming individuals who are able freely and in an informed way to choose and who are prepared themselves to assume responsibility for their choices. There is an obligation imposed upon us all, unlike that we have with respect to animals, to respond to children in such a way as to maximize the chances of their becoming persons. This may well impose upon us the obligation to treat them as persons from a very early age, that is, to respect their choices and to place upon them the responsibility for the choices to be made. There is no need to say that there is a close connection between how we respond to them and what they become. It also imposes upon us all the duty to display constantly the qualities of a person, for what they become they will largely become because of what they learn from us is acceptable behavior. . . .

NOTE

1. "When a man is suffering from an infectious disease, he is a danger to the community, and it is necessary to restrict his liberty of movement. But no one associates any idea of guilt with such a situation. On the contrary, he is an object of commiseration to his friends. Such steps as science recommends are taken to cure him of his disease, and he submits as a rule without reluctance

to the curtailment of liberty involved meanwhile. The same method in spirit ought to be shown in the treatment of what is called 'crime.'"

Bertrand Russell, *Roads to Freedom* (London: George Allen and Unwin Ltd., 1918), p. 135.

"We do not hold people responsible for their reflexes—for example, for coughing in church. We hold them responsible for their operant behavior—for example, for whispering in church or remaining in church while coughing. But there are variables which are responsible for whispering as well as coughing, and these may be just as inexorable. When we recognize this, we are likely to drop the notion of responsibility altogether and with it the doctrine of free will as an inner causal agent."

B. F. Skinner, *Science and Human Behavior* (1953), pp. 115-6.

"Basically, criminality is but a symptom of insanity, using the term in its widest generic sense to express unacceptable social behavior based on unconscious motivation flowing from a disturbed instinctive and emotional life, whether this appears in frank psychoses, or in less obvious form in neuroses and unrecognized psychoses. . . . If criminals are products of early environmental influences in the same sense that psychotics and neurotics are, then it should be possible to reach them psychotherapeutically."

Benjamin Karpman, "Criminal Psychodynamics," *Journal of Criminal Law and Criminology* 47 (1956), p. 9.

"We, the agents of society, must move to end the game of tit-for-tat and blow-for-blow in which the offender has foolishly and futilely engaged himself and us. We are not driven, as he is, to wild and impulsive actions. With knowledge comes power, and with power there is no need for the frightened vengeance of the old penology. In its place should go a quiet, dignified, therapeutic program for the rehabilitation of the disorganized one, if possible, the protection of society during the treatment period, and his guided return to useful citizenship, as soon as this can be effected."

Karl Menninger, "Therapy, Not Punishment," *Harper's Magazine* (August 1959), pp. 63-64. [See the present volume pp. 47-55.]

Part Two

Capital Punishment

The Morality of Anger

Walter Berns

Until recently, my business did not require me to think about the punishment of criminals in general or the legitimacy and efficacy of capital punishment in particular. In a vague way, I was aware of the disagreement among professionals concerning the purpose of punishment—whether it was intended to deter others, to rehabilitate the criminal, or to pay him back— but like most laymen I had no particular reason to decide which purpose was right or to what extent they may all have been right. I did know that retribution was held in ill repute among criminologists and jurists— to them, retribution was a fancy name for revenge, and revenge was barbaric—and, of course, I knew that capital punishment had the support only of policemen, prison guards, and some local politicians, the sort of people Arthur Koestler calls "hanghards" (Philadelphia's Mayor Rizzo comes to mind). The intellectual community denounced it as both unnecessary and immoral. It was the phenomenon of Simon Wiesenthal that allowed me to understand why the intellectuals were wrong and why the police, the politicians, and the majority of the voters were right: We punish criminals principally in order to pay them back, and we execute the worst of them out of moral necessity. Anyone who respects Wiesenthal's mission will be driven to the same conclusion.

Of course, not everyone will respect that mission. It will strike the busy man—I mean the sort of man who sees things only in the light cast by a concern for his own interests—as somewhat bizarre. Why should anyone devote his life—more than thirty years of it!—exclusively to the task of hunting down the Nazi war criminals who survived World War II and escaped punishment? Wiesenthal says his conscience forces him "to bring the guilty ones to trial." But why punish them? What do we hope to accomplish now by punishing SS Obersturmbannfürer Adolf Eichmann or SS Obersturmbannführer Franz Stangl or someday—who knows?—Reichsleiter Martin Bormann? We surely don't expect to rehabilitate them, and it would be foolish to think that by punishing them we might thereby deter others. The answer, I think, is clear: We want to punish them in order *to pay them back.* We think they must be made to pay for their crimes with their lives, and we think that we, the survivors of the world they violated, may legitimately exact that payment because we, too, are their victims. By punishing them, we demonstrate that there are laws that bind men across generations as well as across (and within) nations, that we are not simply isolated individuals, each pursuing his selfish interests and connected with others by a mere contract to live and let live. To state it simply, Wiesenthal allows us to see that it is right, morally right, to be angry with criminals and to express that anger publicly, officially, and in an appropriate manner, which may require the worst of them to be executed.

Modern civil-libertarian opponents of capital punishment do not understand this. They say that to execute a criminal is to deny his human dignity; they also say that the death penalty is not useful, that nothing useful is accomplished by executing anyone. Being utilitarians, they are essentially selfish men, distrustful of passion, who do not understand the connection between anger and justice, and between anger and human dignity.

Anger is expressed or manifested on those occasions when someone has acted in a manner that is thought to be unjust, and one of its origins is the opinion that men are responsible, and should be held responsible, for what they do. Thus, as Aristotle teaches us, anger is accompanied not only by the pain caused by the one who is the object of anger, but by the pleasure arising from the expectation of inflicting revenge on someone who is thought to deserve it. We can become angry with an inanimate object (the door we run into and then kick in return) only by foolishly attributing responsibility to it, and we cannot do that for long, which is why we do not think of returning later to revenge ourselves on the door. For the same reason, we cannot be more than momentarily angry with any one creature other than man; only a fool and worse would dream of taking revenge on a dog. And, finally, we tend to pity rather than to be angry with men who—because they are insane, for example—are not responsible for their acts. Anger, then, is a very human passion not only because only a human being can be angry, but also because anger acknowledges the humanity of its objects: it holds them accountable for what they do. And in holding particular men responsible, it pays them the respect that is due them as men. Anger recognizes that only men have the capacity to be moral beings and, in so doing, acknowledges the dignity of human beings. Anger is somehow connected with justice, and it is this that modern penology has not understood; it tends, on the whole, to regard anger as a selfish indulgence.

Anger can, of course, be that; and if someone does not become angry with an insult or an injury suffered unjustly, we tend to think he does not think much of himself. But it need not be selfish, not in the sense of being provoked only by an injury suffered by oneself. There were many angry men in America when President Kennedy was killed; one of them— Jack Ruby—took it upon himself to exact the punishment that, if indeed deserved, ought to have been exacted by the law. There were perhaps even angrier men when Martin Luther King, Jr., was killed, for King, more than anyone else at the time, embodied a people's quest for justice; the anger—more, the "black rage"—expressed on that occasion was simply a manifestation of the great change that had occurred among black men in America, a change wrought in large part by King and his associates in the civil-rights movement: the servility and fear of the past had been replaced by pride and anger, and the treatment that had formerly been accepted as a matter of course or as if it were deserved was now seen for what it was, unjust and unacceptable. King preached love, but the movement he led depended on anger as well as love, and that anger was not despicable, being neither selfish nor unjustified. On the contrary, it was a reflection of what was called solidarity and may more accurately be called a profound caring for others, black for other blacks, white for blacks, and, in the world King was trying to build, American for other Americans. If men are not saddened when someone else suffers, or angry when someone else suffers unjustly, the implication is that they do not care for anyone other than themselves or that they lack some quality that befits a man. When we criticize them for this, we acknowledge that they ought to care for others. If men are not angry when a neighbor suffers at the hands of a criminal, the implication is that their moral faculties have been corrupted, that they are not good citizens.

Criminals are properly the objects of anger, and the perpetrators of terrible crimes—for example, Lee Harvey Oswald and James Earl Ray— are properly the objects of great anger. They have done more than inflict an injury on an isolated individual; they have violated the foundations of trust and friendship, the necessary elements of a moral community, the only community worth living in. A moral community, unlike a hive of bees or a hill of ants, is one whose members are expected freely to obey the laws and, unlike those in a tyranny, are trusted to obey the laws. The criminal has violated that trust, and in so doing has injured not merely his immediate victim but the community as such. He has called into question the very possibility of that community by suggesting that men cannot be trusted to respect freely the property, the person, and the dignity of those with whom they are associated. If, then, men are not angry when someone else is robbed, raped, or murdered, the implication is that no moral community exists, because those men do not care for anyone other than themselves. Anger is an expression of that caring, and society needs men who care for one another, who share their pleasures and their pains, and do so for the sake of the others. It is the passion that can cause us to act for reasons having nothing to do with selfish or mean calculation; indeed, when educated, it can become a generous passion, the passion that protects the community or country by demanding punishment for its enemies. It is the stuff from which heroes are made.

A moral community is not possible without anger and the moral indignation that accompanies it. Thus the most powerful attack on capital punishment was written by a man, Albert Camus, who denied the legitimacy of anger and moral indignation by denying the very possibility of a moral community in our time. The anger expressed in our world, he said, is nothing but hypocrisy. His novel L'Etranger (variously translated as The Stranger or The Outsider) is a brilliant portrayal of what Camus insisted is our world, a world deprived of God, as he put it. It is a world we would not choose to live in and one that Camus, the hero of the French Resistance, disdained. Nevertheless, the novel is a modern masterpiece, and Meursault, its antihero (for a world without anger can have no heroes), is a murderer.

He is a murderer whose crime is excused, even as his lack of hypocrisy is praised, because the universe, we are told, is "benignly indifferent" to how we live or what we do. Of course, the law is not indifferent; the law punished Meursault and it threatens to punish us if we do as he did. But Camus the novelist teaches us that the law is simply a collection of arbitrary conceits. The people around Meursault apparently were not indifferent; they expressed dismay at his lack of attachment to his mother and disapprobation of his crime. But Camus the novelist teaches us that other people are hypocrites. They pretend not to know what Camus the opponent of capital punishment tells: namely, that "our civilization has lost the only values that, in a certain way, can justify that penalty . . . [the existence of] a truth or a principle that is superior to man." There is no basis for friendship and no moral law; therefore, no one, not even a murderer, can violate the terms of friendship or break that law; and there is no basis for the anger that we express when someone breaks that law. The only thing we share as men, the only thing that connects us one to another, is a "solidarity against death," and a judgment of capital punishment "upsets" that solidarity. The purpose of human life is to stay alive.

Like Meursault, Macbeth was a murderer, and like L'Etranger, Shakespeare's Macbeth is the story of a murder; but there the similarity ends. As Lincoln said, "Nothing equals Macbeth." He was comparing it with the other Shakespearean plays he knew, the plays he had "gone over perhaps as frequently as any unprofessional reader . . . *Lear, Richard Third, Henry Eighth, Hamlet*"; but I think he meant to say more than that none of these equals *Macbeth.* I think he meant that no other literary work equals it. "It is wonderful," he said. *Macbeth* is wonderful because, to say nothing more here, it teaches us the awesomeness of the commandment "Thou shalt not kill."

What can a dramatic poet tell us about murder? More, probably, than anyone else, if he is a poet worthy of consideration, and yet nothing that does not inhere in the act itself. In *Macbeth,* Shakespeare shows us murders committed in a political world by a man so driven by ambition to rule that world that he becomes a tyrant. He shows us also the consequences, which were terrible, worse even than Macbeth feared. The cosmos rebelled, turned into chaos by his deeds. He shows a world that was not "benignly indifferent" to what we call crimes and especially to murder, a world constituted by laws divine as well as human, and Macbeth violated the most awful of those laws. Because the world was so constituted, Macbeth suffered the torments of the great and the damned, torments far beyond the "practice" of any physician. He had known glory and had deserved the respect and affection of king, countrymen, army, friends, and wife; and he lost it all. At the end he was reduced to saying that life "is a tale told by an idiot, full of sound and fury, signifying nothing"; yet, in spite of the horrors provoked in us by his acts, he excites no anger in us. We pity him; even so, we understand the anger of his countrymen and the dramatic necessity of his death. *Macbeth* is a play about ambition, murder, tyranny; about horror, anger, vengeance, and perhaps more than any other of Shakespeare's plays, justice. Because of justice, Macbeth has to die, not by his own hand—he will not "play the Roman fool, and die on [his] sword"—but at the hand of the avenging Macduff. The dramatic necessity of his death would appear to rest on its *moral* necessity. Is that right? Does this play conform to our sense of what a murder means? Lincoln thought it was "wonderful."

Surely Shakespeare's is a truer account of murder than the one provided by Camus, and by truer I mean truer to our moral sense of what a murder is and what the consequences that attend it must be. Shakespeare shows us vengeful men because there is something in the souls of men—then and now—that requires such crimes to be revenged. Can we imagine a world that does not take its revenge on the man who kills Macduff's wife and children? (Can we imagine the play in which Macbeth does not die?) Can we imagine a people that does not hate murderers? (Can we imagine a world where Meursault is an outsider only because he does not *pretend* to be outraged by murder?) Shakespeare's poetry could not have been written out of the moral sense that the death penalty's opponents insist we ought to have. Indeed, the issue of capital punishment can be said to turn on whether Shakespeare's or Camus' is the more telling account of murder.

There is a sense in which punishment may be likened to dramatic poetry. Dramatic poetry depicts men's actions because men are revealed in, or make themselves known through, their actions; and the essence of a human action, according to Aristotle, consists in its being virtuous or vicious. Only a ruler or a contender for rule can act with the freedom and on a scale that allows the virtuousness or viciousness of human deeds to be fully displayed. Macbeth was such a man, and in his fall, brought about by his own acts, and in the consequent suffering he endured, is revealed the meaning of morality. In *Macbeth* the majesty of the moral law is demonstrated to us; as I said, it teaches us the awesomeness of the commandment Thou shalt not kill. In a similar fashion, the punishments imposed by the legal order remind us of the reign of the moral order; not only do they remind us of it, but by enforcing its prescriptions, they enhance the dignity of the legal order in the eyes of moral men, in the eyes of those decent citizens who cry out "for gods who will avenge injustice." That is especially important in a self-governing community, a community that gives laws to itself.

If the laws were understood to be divinely inspired or, in the extreme case, divinely given, they would enjoy all the dignity that the opinions of men can grant and all the dignity they require to ensure their being obeyed by most of the men living under them. Like Duncan in the opinion of Macduff, the laws would be "the Lord's anointed," and would be obeyed even as Macduff obeyed the laws of the Scottish kingdom. Only a Macbeth would challenge them, and only a Meursault would ignore them. But the laws of the United States are not of this description; in fact, among the proposed amendments that became the Bill of Rights was one declaring, not that all power comes from God, but rather "that all power is originally vested in, and consequently derives from the people"; and this proposal was dropped only because it was thought to be redundant: the Constitution's preamble said essentially the same thing, and what we know as the Tenth Amendment reiterated it. So Madison proposed to make the Constitution venerable in the minds of the people, and Lincoln, in an early speech, went so far as to say that a "political religion" should be made of it. They did not doubt that the Constitution and the laws made pursuant to it would be supported by "enlightened reason," but fearing that enlightened reason would be in short supply, they sought to augment it. The laws of the United States would be obeyed by some men because they could hear and understand "the voice of enlightened reason," and by other men because they would regard the laws with that "veneration which time bestows on everthing."

Supreme Court justices have occasionally complained of our habit of making "constitutionality synonymous with wisdom." But the extent to which the Constitution is venerated and its authority accepted depends on the compatibility of its rules with our moral sensibilities; despite its venerable character, the Constitution is not the only source of these moral sensibilities. There was even a period, before slavery was abolished by the Thirteenth Amendment, when the Constitution was regarded by some very moral men as an abomination: Garrison called it "a covenant with death and an agreement with Hell," and there were honorable men holding important political offices and judicial appointments who refused to enforce the Fugitive Slave Law even though its constitutionality had been affirmed. In time this opinion spread far beyond the ranks of the original abolitionists until those who held it composed a constitutional majority of the people, and slavery was abolished.

But Lincoln knew that more than amendments were required to make the Constitution once more worthy of the veneration of moral men. That is why, in the Gettysburg Address, he made the principle of the Constitution an inheritance from "our fathers." That it should be so esteemed is especially important in a self-governing nation that gives laws to itself, because it is only a short step from the principle that the laws are merely a product of one's own will to the opinion that the only consideration that informs the law is self-interest; and this opinion is only one remove from lawlessness. A nation of simple self-interested men will soon enough perish from the earth.

It was not an accident that Lincoln spoke as he did at Gettysburg or that he chose as the occasion for his words the dedication of a cemetery built on a portion of the most significant battlefield of the Civil War. Two-and-a-half years earlier, in his First Inaugural Address, he had said that Americans, north and south, were not and must not be enemies, but friends. Passion had strained but must not be allowed to break the bonds of affection that tied them one to another. He closed by saying this: "The mystic chords of memory, stretching from every battlefield, and patriot grave, to every living heart and hearthstone, all over this broad land, will yet swell the chorus of the Union, when again touched, as surely they will be, by the better angels of our nature." The chords of memory that would swell the chorus of the Union could be touched, even by a man of Lincoln's stature, only on the most solemn occasions, and in the life of a nation no occasion is more solemn than the burial of the patriots who have died defending it on the field of battle. War is surely an evil, but as Hegel said, it is not an "absolute evil." It exacts the supreme sacrifice, but precisely because of that it can call forth such sublime rhetoric as Lincoln's. His words at Gettysburg serve to remind Americans in particular of what Hegel said people in general needed to know, and could be made to know by means of war and the sacrifices demanded of them in wars: namely, that their country is something more than a "civil society" the purpose of which is simply the protection of individual and selfish interests.

Capital punishment, like Shakespeare's dramatic and Lincoln's political poetry (and it is surely that, and was understood by him to be that), serves to remind us of the majesty of the moral order that is embodied in our law, and of the terrible consequences of its breach. The law must not be understood to be merely a statute that we enact or repeal at our will, and obey or disobey at our convenience—especially not the criminal law. Wherever law is regarded as merely statutory, men will soon enough disobey it, and will learn how to do so without any inconvenience to themselves. The criminal law must possess a dignity far beyond that possessed by mere statutory enactment or utilitarian and self-interested calculations. The most powerful means we have to give it that dignity is to authorize it to impose the ultimate penalty. The criminal law must be made awful, by which I mean inspiring, or commanding "profound respect or reverential fear." It must remind us of the moral order by which alone we can live as *human* beings, and in America, now that the Supreme Court has outlawed banishment, the only punishment that can do this is capital punishment.

The founder of modern criminology, the eighteenth-century Italian Cesare Beccaria, opposed both banishment and capital punishment because he understood that both were inconsistent with the principle of self-interest, and self-interest was the basis of the political order he favored. If a man's first or only duty is to himself, of course he will prefer his money to his country; he will also prefer his money to his brother. In fact, he will prefer his brother's money to his brother, and a people of this description, or a country that understands itself in this Beccarian manner, can put the mark of Cain on no one. For the same reason, such a country can have no legitimate reason to execute its criminals, or, indeed, to punish them in any manner. What would be accomplished by punishment in such a place? Punishment arises out of the demand for justice, and justice is demanded by angry, morally indignant men; its purpose is to satisfy that moral indignation and thereby promote the law-abidingness that, it is assumed, accompanies it. But the principle of self-interest denies the moral basis of that indignation.

Not only will a country based solely on self-interest have no legitimate reason to punish; it may have no need to punish. It may be able to solve what we call the crime problem by substituting a law of contracts for a law of crimes. According to Beccaria's social contract, men agree to yield their natural freedom to the "sovereign" in exchange for his promise to keep the peace. As it becomes more difficult for the sovereign to fulfill his part of the contract, there is a demand that he be made to pay for his nonperformance. From this comes compensation or insurance schemes embodied in statutes whereby the sovereign (or state), being unable to keep the peace by punishing criminals, agrees to compensate its contractual partners for injuries suffered at the hands of criminals, injuries the police are unable to prevent. The insurance policy takes the place of law enforcement and the *posse comitatus,* and John Wayne and Gary Cooper give way to Mutual of Omaha. There is no anger in this kind of law, and none (or no reason for any) in the society. The principle can be carried further still. If we ignore the victim (and nothing we do can restore his life anyway), there would appear to be no reason why—the worth of a man being his price, as Beccaria's teacher, Thomas Hobbes, put it—coverage should not be extended to the losses incurred in a murder. If we ignore the victim's sensibilities (and what are they but absurd vanities?), there would appear to be no reason why—the worth of a woman being *her* price—coverage should not be extended to the losses incurred in a rape. Other examples will no doubt suggest themselves.

This might appear to be an almost perfect solution to what we persist in calling the crime problem, achieved without risking the terrible things sometimes done by an angry people. A people that is not angry with criminals will not be able to deter crime, but a people fully covered by insurance has no need to deter crime: they will be insured against all the losses they can, in principle, suffer. What is now called crime can be expected to increase in volume, of course, and this will cause an increase in the premiums paid, directly or in the form of taxes. But it will no longer be necessary to apprehend, try, and punish criminals, which now costs Americans more than $1.5 billion a month (and is increasing at an annual rate of about 15 percent), and one can buy a lot of insurance for $1.5 billion. There is this difficulty, as Rousseau put it: To exclude anger from the human community is to concentrate all the passions in a "self-interest of the meanest sort," and such a place would not be fit for human habitation.

When, in 1976, the Supreme Court declared death to be a constitutional penalty, it decided that the United States was not that sort of country; most of us, I think, can appreciate that judgment. We want to live among people who do not value their possessions more than their citizenship, who do not think exclusively or even primarily of their own rights, people whom we can depend on even as they exercise their rights, and whom we can trust, which is to say, people who, even in the absence of a policeman, will not assault our bodies or steal our possessions, and might even come to our assistance when we need it, and who stand ready, when the occasion demands it, to risk their lives in defense of their country. If we are of the opinion that the United States may rightly ask of its citizens this awful sacrifice, then we are also of the opinion that it may rightly impose the most awful penalty; if it may rightly honor its heroes, it may rightly execute the worst of its criminals. By doing so, it will remind its citizens that it is a country worthy of heroes.

Does It Matter If the Death Penalty Is Arbitrarily Administered?

Stephen Nathanson

I

In this article, I will examine the argument that capital punishment ought to be abolished because it has been and will continue to be imposed in an arbitrary manner.

This argument has been central to discussions of capital punishment since the Supreme Court ruling in the 1972 case *Furman v. Georgia*. In a 5-4 decision, the Court ruled that capital punishment as then administered was unconstitutional. Although the Court issued several opinions, the problem of arbitrariness is widely seen as having played a central role in the Court's thinking. As Charles Black, Jr., has put it,

> ... The decisive ground of the 1972 Furman case anti-capital punishment ruling—the ground persuasive to the marginal justices needed for a majority—was that, out of a large number of persons "eligible" in law for the punishment of death, a few were selected as if at random, by no stated (or perhaps statable) criteria, while all the rest suffered the lesser penalty of imprisonment.[1]

Among those justices moved by the arbitrariness issue, some stressed the discriminatory aspects of capital punishment, the tendency of legally irrelevant factors like race and economic status to determine the severity of sentence, while others emphasized the "freakish" nature of the punishment, the fact that it is imposed on a miniscule percentage of murderers who are not obviously more deserving of death than others.

From *Philosophy & Public Affairs* 14, no. 2 (Spring 1985). Copyright © 1985 by Princeton University Press. Reprinted with permission of Princeton University Press.

Although the Supreme Court approved new death penalty laws in *Gregg v. Georgia* (1976), the reasoning of *Furman* was not rejected. Rather, a majority of the Court determined that Georgia's new laws would make arbitrary imposition of the death penalty much less likely. By amending procedures and adding criteria which specify aggravating and mitigating circumstances, Georgia had succeeded in creating a system of "guided discretion," which the Court accepted in the belief that it was not likely to yield arbitrary results.

The *Gregg* decision has prompted death penalty opponents to attempt to show that "guided discretion" is an illusion. This charge has been supported in various ways. Charles Black has supported it by analyzing both the legal process of decision making in capital cases and the legal criteria for determining who is to be executed. He has argued that, appearances to the contrary, there are no meaningful standards operating in the system. Attacking from an empirical angle, William Bowers and Glenn Pierce have tried to show that even after *Furman* and under new laws, factors like race and geographic location of the trial continue to play a large role and that the criteria which are supposed to guide judgment do not separate those sentenced into meaningfully distinct groups. Perhaps the most shocking conclusion of Bowers and Pierce concerns the large role played by the race of the killer and the victims, as the chances of execution are by far the greatest when blacks kill whites and least when whites kill blacks.[2]

The upshot of both these approaches is that "guided discretion" is not working and, perhaps, cannot work. If this is correct and if the argument from arbitrariness is accepted, then it would appear that a return from *Gregg* to *Furman* is required. That is, the Court should once again condemn capital punishment as unconstitutional.

I have posed these issues in terms of the Supreme Court's deliberations. Nonetheless, for opponents of the death penalty, the freakishness of its imposition and the large role played by race and other irrelevant factors are a moral as well as a legal outrage. For them, there is a fundamental moral injustice in the practice of capital punishment and not just a departure from the highest legal and constitutional standards.

II

The argument from arbitrariness has not, however, been universally accepted, either as a moral or a constitutional argument. Ernest van den Haag, an articulate and longtime defender of the death penalty, has claimed that the Supreme Court was wrong to accept this argument in the first place and thus that the evidence of arbitrariness presented by Black, Bowers and Pierce and others is beside the point. In his words:

... the abolitionist argument from capriciousness, or discretion, or discrimination, would be more persuasive if it were alleged that those selectively executed are not guilty. But the argument merely maintains that some other guilty but more favored persons, or groups, escape the death penalty. This is hardly sufficient for letting anyone else found guilty escape the penalty. On the contrary, that some guilty persons or groups elude it argues for extending the death penalty to them.[3]

Having attacked the appeal to arbitrariness, van den Haag goes on to spell out his own conception of the requirements of justice. He writes:

> Justice requires punishing the guilty—as many of the guilty as possible, even if only some can be punished—and sparing the innocent—as many of the innocent as possible, even if not all are spared. It would surely be wrong to treat everybody with equal injustice in preference to meting out justice at least to some. . . . [I]f the death penalty is morally just, *however discriminatorily applied to only some of the guilty,* it does remain just *in each case* in which it is applied. (emphasis added)[4]

Distinguishing sharply between the demands of justice and the demands of equality, van den Haag claims that the justice of individual punishments depends on individual guilt alone and not on whether punishments are equally distributed among the class of guilty persons.

Van den Haag's distinction between the demands of justice and the demands of equality parallels the distinction drawn by Joel Feinberg between "noncomparative" and "comparative" justice.[5] Using Feinberg's terminology, we can express van den Haag's view by saying that he believes that the justice of a particular punishment is a *noncomparative* matter. It depends solely on what a person deserves and not on how others are treated. For van den Haag, then, evidence of arbitrariness and discrimination is irrelevant, so long as those who are executed are indeed guilty and deserve their punishment.

There is no denying the plausibility of van den Haag's case. In many instances, we believe it is legitimate to punish or reward deserving individuals, even though we know that equally deserving persons are unpunished or unrewarded. Consider two cases:

> A. A driver is caught speeding, ticketed, and required to pay a fine. We know that the percentage of speeders who are actually punished is extremely small, yet we would probably regard it as a joke if the driver protested that he was being treated unjustly or if someone argued that no one should be fined for speeding unless all speeders were fined.

> B. A person performs a heroic act and receives a substantial reward, in addition to the respect and admiration of his fellow citizens. Because

he deserves the reward, we think it just that he receive it, even though many equally heroic persons are not treated similarly. That most heroes are unsung is no reason to avoid rewarding this particular heroic individual.

Both of these instances appear to support van den Haag's claim that we should do justice whenever we can in individual cases and that failure to do justice in all cases is no reason to withhold punishment or reward from individuals.

III

Is the argument from arbitrariness completely unfounded then? Should we accept van den Haag's claim that "unequal justice is justice still"?

In response to these questions, I shall argue that van den Haag's case is not as strong as it looks and that the argument from arbitrariness can be vindicated.

As a first step in achieving this, I would like to point out that there are in fact several different arguments from arbitrariness. While some of these arguments appeal to the random and freakish nature of the death penalty, others highlight the discriminatory effects of legally irrelevant factors. Each of these kinds of arbitrariness raises different sorts of moral and legal issues.

For example, though we may acknowledge the impossibility of ticketing all speeding drivers and still favor ticketing some, we will not find every way of determining which speeders are ticketed equally just. Consider the policy of ticketing only those who travel at extremely high speeds, as opposed to that of ticketing every tenth car. Compare these with the policy of giving tickets only to speeders with beards and long hair or to speeders whose cars bear bumper stickers expressing unpopular political views. While I shall not pursue this point in detail, I take it to be obvious that these different selection policies are not all equally just or acceptable.

A second difference between versions of the argument from arbitrariness depends on whether or not it is granted that we can accurately distinguish those who deserve to die from those who do not. As van den Haag presents the argument, it assumes that we are able to make this distinction. Then, the claim is made that from this class of people who deserve to die, only some are selected for execution. The choice of those specific persons from the general class of persons who deserve to die is held to be arbitrary.

Van den Haag neglects a related argument which has been forcefully defended by Charles Black. Black's argument is that the determination of *who* deserves to die—the first step—is itself arbitrary. So his claim is not merely that arbitrary factors determine who among the deserving will be executed. His point is that the determination of who deserves to die is arbitrary. His main argument is that

> the official choices—by prosecutors, judges, juries, and governors—that divide those who are to die from those who are to live are on the whole not made, and cannot be made, under standards that are consistently meaningful and clear, but that they are often made, and in the foreseeable future will continue often to be made, under no standards at all or under pseudo-standards without discoverable meaning.[6]

According to Black, even the most conscientious officials could not make principled judgments about desert in these instances, because our laws do not contain clear principles for differentiating those who deserve to die from those who do not. While I shall not try to summarize Black's analysis of the failures of post-*Furman* capital punishment statutes, it is clear that if van den Haag were to meet this argument, he would have to provide his own analysis of these laws in order to show that they do provide clear and meaningful standards. Or, he would have to examine the actual disposition of cases under these laws to show that the results have not been arbitrary. Van den Haag does not attempt to do either of these things. This seems to result from a failure to distinguish (a) the claim that judgments concerning *who deserves to die* are arbitrarily made, from (b) the claim that judgments concerning *who among the deserving shall be executed* are arbitrarily made.

Van den Haag may simply assume that the system does a decent job of distinguishing those who deserve to die from those who do not, and his assumption gains a surface plausibility because of his tendency to oversimplify the nature of the judgments which need to be made. In contrast to Black, who stresses the complexity of the legal process and the complexity of the judgments facing participants in that process, van den Haag is content to say simply that "justice requires punishing the guilty . . . and sparing the innocent." This maxim makes it look as if officials and jurors need only divide people into two neat categories, and if we think of guilt and innocence as *factual* categories, it makes it look as if the only judgment necessary is whether a person did or did not kill another human being.

In fact, the problems are much more complicated than this. Not every person who kills another human being is guilty of the same crime. Some may have committed no crime at all, if their act is judged to be justifiable homicide. Among others, they may have committed first-degree murder, second-degree murder, or some form of manslaughter. Furthermore, even if we limit our attention to those who are convicted of first-degree murder, juries must consider aggravating and mitigating circumstances in order to judge whether someone is guilty enough to deserve the death penalty. It is clear, then, that simply knowing that someone is factually guilty of killing another person is far from sufficient for determining that he deserves to die, and if prosecutors, juries, and judges do not have criteria which enable them to classify those who are guilty in a just and rational way, then their judgments about who deserves to die will necessarily be arbitrary and unprincipled.

Once we appreciate the difficulty and complexity of the judgments which must be made about guilt and desert, it is easier to see how they might be influenced by racial characteristics and other irrelevant factors. The statistics compiled by Bowers and Pierce show that blacks killing whites have the greatest chance of being executed, while whites killing blacks have the least chance of execution. What these findings strongly suggest is that officials and jurors think that the killing of a white by a black is a more serious crime than the killing of a black by a white. Hence, they judge that blacks killing whites *deserve* a more serious punishment than whites killing blacks. Given the bluntness of our ordinary judgments about desert and the complexity of the choices facing jurors and officials, it may not be surprising either that people find it difficult to make the fine discriminations required by law or that such judgments are influenced by deep-seated racial or social attitudes.

Both legal analysis and empirical studies should undermine our confidence that the legal system sorts out those who deserve to die from those who do not in a nonarbitrary manner. If we cannot be confident that those who are executed in fact deserve to die, then we ought not to allow executions to take place at all.

Because van den Haag does not distinguish this argument from other versions of the argument from arbitrariness, he simply neglects it. His omission is serious because this argument is an independent, substantial argument against the death penalty. It can stand even if other versions of the argument from arbitrariness fall.

IV

I would like now to turn to the form of the argument which van den Haag explicitly deals with and to consider whether it is vulnerable to his criticisms. Let us assume that there is a class of people whom we know to be deserving of death. Let us further assume that only some of these people are executed and that the executions are arbitrary in the sense that those executed have not committed worse crimes than those not executed. This is the situation which Justice Stewart described in *Furman*. He wrote:

These death sentences are cruel and unusual in the same way that being struck by lightning is cruel and unusual. For of all the people convicted of rapes and murders in 1967 and 1968, *many just as reprehensible as these,* the petitioners are among *a capriciously selected random handful* upon whom the sentence of death has in fact been imposed. (emphasis added)[7]

What is crucial here (and different from the argument previously discussed) is the assumption that we can judge the reprehensibility of both the petitioners and others convicted of similar crimes. Stewart does not deny that the petitioners deserve to die, but because other equally deserving people escape the death penalty for no legally respectable reasons, the executions of the petitioners, Stewart thought, would violate the Eighth and Fourteenth Amendments.

This is precisely the argument van den Haag rejected. We can sum up his reasons in the following rhetorical questions: How can it possibly be unjust to punish someone if he deserves the punishment? Why should it matter whether or not others equally deserving are punished?

I have already acknowledged the plausibility of van den Haag's case and offered the examples of the ticketed speeder and the rewarded hero as instances which seem to confirm his view. Nonetheless, I think that van den Haag is profoundly mistaken in thinking that the justice of a reward or punishment depends solely on whether the recipient deserves it.

Consider the following two cases which are structurally similar to A and B (given above) but which elicit different reactions:

C. I tell my class that anyone who plagiarizes will fail the course. Three students plagiarize papers, but only one receives a failing grade. The other two, in describing their motivation, win my sympathy, and I give them passing grades.

D. At my child's birthday party, I offer a prize to the child who can solve a particular puzzle. Three children, including my own, solve the puzzle. I cannot reward them all, so I give the prize to my own child.

In both cases, as in van den Haag's, only some of those deserving a reward or punishment receive it. Unlike cases A and B, however, C and D do not appear to be just, in spite of the fact that the persons rewarded or punished deserve what they get. In these cases, the justice of giving them what they deserve appears to be affected by the treatment of others.

About these cases I am inclined to say the following. The people involved have not been treated justly. It was unjust to fail the single plagiarizer and unjust to reward my child. It would have been better—

because more just—to have failed no one than to have failed the single student. I would have been better to have given a prize to no one than to give the prize to my child alone.

The unfairness in both cases appears to result from the fact that the reasons for picking out those rewarded or punished are irrelevant and hence that the choice is arbitrary. If I have a stated policy of failing students who plagiarize, then it is unjust for me to pass students with whom I sympathize. Whether I am sympathetic or not is irrelevant, and I am treating the student whom I do fail unjustly because I am not acting simply on the basis of desert. Rather, I am acting on the basis of desert plus degree of sympathy. Likewise, in the case of the prize, it appears that I am preferring my own child in giving out the reward, even though I announced that receipt of the award would depend only on success in solving the puzzle.

This may be made clearer by varying the plagiarism example. Suppose that in spite of my stated policy of failing anyone who plagiarizes, I am regularly lenient toward students who seem sufficiently repentant. Suppose further that I am regularly more lenient with attractive female students than with others. Or suppose that it is only redheads or wealthy students whom I fail. If such patterns develop, we can see that whether a student fails or not does not depend simply on being caught plagiarizing. Rather, part of the explanation of a particular student's being punished is that he or she is (or is not) an attractive female, redheaded or wealthy. In these instances, I think the plagiarizers who are punished have grounds for complaint, even though they were, by the announced standards, clearly guilty and deserving of punishment.

If this conclusion is correct, then doing justice is more complicated than van den Haag realizes. He asserts that it would be "wrong to treat everybody with equal injustice in preference to meting out justice at least to some." If my assessment of cases C and D is correct, however, it is better that everyone in those instances be treated "unjustly" than that only some get what they deserve. Whether one is treated justly or not depends on how others are treated and not solely on what one deserves.[8]

In fact, van den Haag implicitly concedes this point in an interesting footnote to his essay. In considering the question of whether capital punishment is a superior deterrent, van den Haag mentions that one could test the deterrent power of the death penalty by allowing executions for murders committed on Monday, Wednesday, and Friday, while setting life imprisonment as the maximum penalty for murders committed on other days. In noting the obstacles facing such an experiment, he writes:

> . . . it is not acceptable to our sense of justice that *people guilty of the same crime would get different punishments* and that the difference would

be made to depend deliberately on *a factor irrelevant to the nature of the crime* or of the criminal. (emphasis added)[9]

Given his earlier remarks about the argument from arbitrariness, this is a rather extraordinary comment, for van den Haag concedes that the justice of a punishment is not solely determined by what an individual deserves but is also a function of how equally deserving persons are treated in general.

In his case, what he finds offensive is that there is no difference between what the Monday, Wednesday, Friday murderers deserve and what the Tuesday, Thursday, Saturday, and Sunday murderers deserve. Yet the morally irrelevant factor of date is decisive in determining the severity of the punishment. Van den Haag (quite rightly) cannot swallow this.

Yet van den Haag's example is exactly parallel to the situation described by opponents of the death penalty. For, surely, the race of the criminal or victim, the economic or social status of the criminal or victim, the location of the crime or trial and other such factors are as irrelevant to the gravity of the crime and the appropriate severity of the punishment as is the day of the week on which the crime is committed. It would be as outrageous for the severity of the punishment to depend on these factors as it would be for it to depend on the day of the week on which the crime was committed.

In fact, it is more outrageous that death sentences depend on the former factors because a person can control the day of the week on which he murders in a way in which he cannot control his race or status. Moreover, we are committed to banishing the disabling effects of race and economic status from the law. Using the day of the week as a critical factor is at least not invidiously discriminatory, as it neither favors nor disfavors previously identifiable or disadvantaged groups.

In reply, one might contend that I have overlooked an important feature of van den Haag's example. He rejected the deterrence experiment not merely because the severity of punishment depended on irrelevant factors but also because the irrelevant factors were *deliberately* chosen as the basis of punishment. Perhaps it is the fact that irrelevant factors are deliberately chosen which makes van den Haag condemn the proposed experiment.

This is an important point. It certainly makes matters worse to decide deliberately to base life and death choices on irrelevant considerations. However, even if the decision is not deliberate, it remains a serious injustice if irrelevant considerations play this crucial role. Individuals might not even be aware of the influence of these factors. They might genuinely believe that their judgments are based entirely on relevant considerations. It might require painstaking research to discover the patterns underlying sentencing, but once they are known, citizens and policymakers must take them into consideration. Either the influence of irrelevant factors must be eradicated or, if we determine that this is impossible, we may have to alter our practices more radically.

This reasoning, of course, is just the reasoning identified with the *Furman* case. As Justice Douglas wrote:

> A law that stated that anyone making more than $50,000 would be exempt from the death penalty would plainly fall, as would a law that in terms said that blacks, those who never went beyond the fifth grade in school, those who make less than $3,000 a year, or those who were unpopular or unstable should be the only people executed. A law which in the overall view reaches the same result in practice has no more sanctity than a law which in terms provides the same.[10]

The problem, in Douglas's view, was that the system left life and death decisions to the "uncontrolled discretion of judges or juries," leading to the unintended but nonetheless real result that death sentences were based on factors which had nothing to do with the nature of the crime.

What I want to stress here is that the arbitrariness and discrimination need not be purposeful or deliberate. We might discover, as critics allege, that racial prejudice is so deeply rooted in our society that prosecutors, juries, and judges cannot free themselves from prejudice when determining how severe a punishment for a crime should be. Furthermore, we might conclude that these tendencies cannot be eradicated, especially when juries are called upon to make subtle and complex assessments of cases in the light of confusing, semi-technical criteria. Hence, although no one *decides* that race will be a factor, we may *predict* that it will be a factor, and this knowledge must be considered in evaluating policies and institutions.

If factors *as irrelevant as* the day of the crime determine whether people shall live or die and if the influence of these factors is ineradicable, then we must conclude that we cannot provide a just system of punishment and even those who are guilty and deserving of the most severe punishments (like the Monday killers in van den Haag's experiment) will have a legitimate complaint that they have been treated unjustly.

I conclude, then, that the treatment of *classes* of people is relevant to determining the justice of punishments for *individuals* and van den Haag is wrong to dismiss the second form of the argument from arbitrariness. That argument succeeds in showing that capital punishment is unjust and thus provides a powerful reason for abolishing it.

V

Supporters of the death penalty might concede that serious questions of justice are raised by the influence of arbitrary factors and still deny that this shows that capital punishment ought to be abolished. They could argue that some degree of arbitrariness is present throughout the system of legal punishment, that it is unreasonable to expect our institutions to be perfect, and that acceptance of the argument from arbitrariness would commit us to abolishing all punishment.

In fact, van den Haag makes just these points in his essay. He writes:

> The Constitution, though it enjoins us to minimize capriciousness, does not enjoin a standard of unattainable perfection or exclude penalties because that standard has not been attained. . . . I see no more merit in the attempt to persuade the courts to let all capital-crime defendants go free of capital punishment because some have wrongly escaped it than I see in an attempt to persuade the courts to let all burglars go because some have wrongly escaped imprisonment.[11]

It is an important feature of this objection that it could be made even by one who conceded the injustice of arbitrarily administered death sentences. Rather than agreeing that capital punishment should be abolished, however, this objection moves from the premise that the flaws revealed in capital punishment are shared by *all* punishments to the conclusion that we must either (a) reject all punishments (because of the influence of arbitrary factors on them) or (b) reject the idea that arbitrariness provides a sufficient ground for abolishing the death penalty.

Is there a way out of this dilemma for death penalty opponents?

I believe that there is. Opponents of the death penalty may continue to support other punishments, even though their administration also involves arbitrariness. This is not to suggest, of course, that we should be content with arbitrariness or discrimination in the imposition of any punishment.[12] Rather the point is to emphasize that the argument from arbitrariness counts against the death penalty with special force. There are two reasons for this.

First, death is a much more severe punishment than imprisonment. This is universally acknowledged by advocates and opponents of the death penalty alike. It is recognized in the law by the existence of special procedures for capital cases. Death obliterates the person, depriving him or her of life and thereby, among other things, depriving him or her of any further rights of legal appeal, should new facts be discovered or new understandings of the law be reached. In this connection, it is worth recalling that many people were executed and are now dead because they were tried and sentenced under the pre-*Furman* laws which allowed the "uncontrolled discretion of judges and juries."

Second, though death is the most severe punishment in our legal system, it appears to be unnecessary for protecting citizens, while punishments generally are thought to promote our safety and well-being. The contrast between death and other punishments can be brought out by asking two questions. What would happen if we abolished all punishments? And, what would happen if we abolished the death penalty?

Most of us believe that if all punishments were abolished, there would be social chaos, a Hobbesian war of all against all. To do away with punishment entirely would be to do away with the criminal law and the system of constraints which it supports. Hence, even though the system is not a just one, we believe that we must live with it and strive to make it as fair as possible. On the other hand, if we abolish capital punishment, there is reason to believe that nothing will happen. There is simply no compelling evidence that capital punishment prevents murders better than long-term prison sentences. Indeed, some evidence even suggests that capital punishment increases the number of murders. While I cannot review the various empirical studies of these questions here, I think it can plausibly be asserted that the results of abolishing punishment generally would be disastrous, while the results of abolishing capital punishment are likely to be insignificant.[13]

I conclude then that the argument from arbitrariness has special force against the death penalty because of its extreme severity and its likely uselessness. The arbitrariness of other punishments may be outweighed by their necessity, but the same cannot be said for capital punishment.

VI

In closing, I would like to comment briefly on one other charge made by van den Haag, the charge that the argument from arbitrariness is a "sham" argument because it is not the real reason why people oppose the death penalty. Those who use this argument, van den Haag claims, would oppose capital punishment even if it were not arbitrarily imposed.

At one level, this charge is doubly fallacious. The suggestion of dishonesty introduced by the word "sham" makes the argument into an *ad hominem*. In addition, the charge suggests that there cannot be more than one reason in support of a view. There are many situations in which we offer arguments and yet would not change our view if the argument were refuted, not because the argument is a sham, but because we have additional grounds for what we believe.

Nonetheless, van den Haag's charge may indicate a special difficulty for the argument from arbitrariness, for the argument may well strike people as artificial and legalistic. Somehow, one may feel that it does not deal with the real issues—the wrongness of killing, deterrence, and whether murderers deserve to die.

Part of the problem, I think, is that our ordinary moral thinking involves specific forms of conduct or general rules of personal behavior. The argument from arbitrariness deals with a feature of an *institution,* and thinking about institutions seems to raise difficulties for many people. Believing that an individual murderer deserves to die for a terrible crime, they infer that there ought to be capital punishment, without attending to all of the implications for other individuals which will follow from setting up this practice.

The problem is similar to one that John Stuart Mill highlighted in *On Liberty.* For many people, the fact that an act is wrong is taken to be sufficient ground for its being made illegal. Mill argued against the institutionalization of all moral judgments, and his argument still strikes many people as odd. If the act is wrong, they ask, shouldn't we do everything in our power to stop it? What they fail to appreciate, however, are all of the implications of institutionalizing such judgments.

Likewise, people ask, If so and so deserves to die, shouldn't we empower the state to execute him? The problem, however—or one of many problems—is that institutionalizing this judgment about desert yields a system which makes neither moral nor legal sense. Moreover, it perpetuates and exacerbates the liabilities and disadvantages which unjustly befall many of our fellow citizens. These are genuine and serious problems, and those who have raised them in the context of the capital punishment debate have both exposed troubling facts about the actual workings of the criminal law and illuminated the difficulties of acting justly. Most importantly, they have produced a powerful argument against authorizing the state to use death as a punishment for crime.

NOTES

1. *Capital Punishment: The Inevitability of Caprice and Mistake.* 2d ed. (New York: W. W. Norton & Co., 1981), p. 20.

2. Ibid., *passim;* W. Bowers and G. Pierce, "Arbitrariness and Discrimination under Post-*Furman* Capital Statutes," *Crime & Delinquency* 26 (1980): 563-635. Reprinted in *The Death Penalty in America,* 3d ed., ed. Hugo Bedau (New York: Oxford University Press, 1982), pp. 206-24.

3. "The Collapse of the Case Against Capital Punishment," *National Review,* 31 March 1978, 397. A briefer version of this paper appeared in the *Criminal Law Bulletin* 14 (1978): 51-68 and is reprinted in Bedau, pp. 323-33.

4. Ibid.

5. "Noncomparative Justice," in *Rights, Justice, and the Bounds of Liberty: Essays in Social Philosophy* (Princeton, NJ: Princeton University Press, 1980); originally published in the *Philosophical Review* 83 (1974): 297-338.

6. Black, *Capital Punishment*, p. 29.

7. Reprinted in Bedau, pp. 263-64.

8. Using Feinberg's terminology, these can be described as cases in which the criteria of comparative and noncomparative justice conflict with one another. I am arguing that in these instances, the criteria of comparative justice take precedence. Although Feinberg does discuss such conflicts, it is unclear to me from his essay whether he would agree with this claim.

9. Van den Haag, "The Collapse of the Case Against Capital Punishment," p. 403, n. 14. (This important footnote does not appear in the shorter version of the paper.)

10. Reprinted in Bedau, pp. 255-56.

11. Van den Haag, "The Collapse of the Case Against Capital Punishment," p. 397.

12. For a discussion of the role of discrimination throughout the criminal justice system and recommendations for reform, see American Friends Service Committee, *Struggle for Justice* (New York: Hill and Wang, 1971).

13. In support of the superior deterrent power of the death penalty, van den Haag cites I. Ehrlich, "The Deterrent Effect of Capital Punishment: A Question of Life and Death," *American Economic Review* 65 (1975): 397-417. Two reviews of the evidence on deterrence, both of which criticize Ehrlich at length, are Hans Zeisel, "The Deterrent Effect of the Death Penalty: Facts v. Faith," and Lawrence Klein et al., "The Deterrent Effect of Capital Punishment: An Assessment of the Evidence." (Both of these articles appear in Bedau.) The thesis that executions increase the number of homicides is defended by W. Bowers and G. Pierce in "Deterrence or Brutalization: What is the Effect of Executions?," *Crime & Delinquency* 26 (1980): 453-84.

My thanks are due to Hugo Bedau, William Bowers, Richard Daynard, and Ernest van den Haag for reactions to my thinking about the death penalty. I would especially like to thank Ursula Bentele for helpful discussions and access to unpublished research, Nelson Lande for spirited comments (both philosophical and grammatical), and John Troyer, whose keen and persistent criticisms of my views forced me to write this article.

Justice, Civilization, and the Death Penalty: Answering van den Haag

Jeffrey H. Reiman

On the issue of capital punishment, there is as clear a clash of moral intuitions as we are likely to see. Some (now a majority of Americans) feel deeply that justice requires payment in kind and thus that murderers should die; and others (once, but no longer, nearly a majority of Americans) feel deeply that the state ought not be in the business of putting people to death.[1] Arguments for either side that do not do justice to the intuitions of the other are unlikely to persuade anyone not already convinced. And, since, as I shall suggest, there is truth on both sides, such arguments are easily refutable, leaving us with nothing but conflicting intuitions and no guidance from reason in distinguishing the better from the worse. In this context, I shall try to make an argument for the abolition of the death penalty that does justice to the intuitions on both sides. I shall sketch out a conception of retributive justice that accounts for the justice of executing murderers, and then I shall argue that *though the death penalty is a just punishment for murder,* abolition of the death penalty is part of the civilizing mission of modern states. Before getting to this, let us briefly consider the challenges confronting those who would argue against the death penalty. In my view, these challenges have been most forcefully put by Ernest van den Haag.

From *Philosophy & Public Affairs* 14, no. 2 (Spring 1985). Copyright © 1985 by Princeton University Press. Reprinted with permission of Princeton University Press.

I. THE CHALLENGE TO THE ABOLITIONIST

The recent book, *The Death Penalty: A Debate*, in which van den Haag argues for the death penalty and John P. Conrad argues against, proves how difficult it is to mount a telling argument against capital punishment.[2] Conrad contends, for example, that "To kill the offender [who has committed murder in the first degree] is to respond to his wrong by doing the same wrong to him" (p. 60). But this popular argument is easily refuted.[3] Since we regard killing in self-defense or in war as morally permissible, it cannot be that we regard killing per se as wrong. It follows that the wrong in murder cannot be that it is killing per se, but that it is (among other things) the killing of an innocent person. Consequently, if the state kills a murderer, though it does the same physical act that he did, it does not do the wrong that he did, since the state is not killing an innocent person (see p. 62). Moreover, unless this distinction is allowed, all punishments are wrong, since everything that the state does as punishment is an act which is physically the same as an act normally thought wrong. For example, if you lock an innocent person in a cage, that is kidnapping. If the state responds by locking you in prison, it can hardly be said to be responding to your wrong by doing you a wrong in return. Indeed, it will be said that it is precisely because what you did was wrong that locking you up, which would otherwise be wrong, is right.[4]

Conrad also makes the familiar appeal to the possibility of executing an innocent person and the impossibility of correcting this tragic mistake. "An act by the state of such monstrous proportions as the execution of a man who is not guilty of the crime for which he was convicted should be avoided at all costs. . . . The abolition of capital punishment is the certain means of preventing the worst injustice" (p. 60). This argument, while not so easily disposed of as the previous one, is, like all claims about what "should be avoided at all costs," neither very persuasive. There is invariably some cost that is prohibitive such that if, for example, capital punishment were necessary to save the lives of potential murder victims, there must be a point at which the number of saved victims would be large enough to justify the risk of executing an innocent—particularly where trial and appellate proceedings are designed to reduce this risk to a minimum by giving the accused every benefit of the doubt.[5] Since we tolerate the death of innocents, in mines or on highways, as a cost of progress, and, in wars, as an inevitable accompaniment to aerial bombardment and the like, it cannot convincingly be contended that, kept to a minimum, the risk of executing an innocent is still so great an evil as to outweigh all other considerations (see pp. 230-31).

Nor will it do to suggest, as Conrad does, that execution implies that offenders are incapable of change and thus presumes the offenders' "total identification with evil," a presumption reserved only to God or, in any case, beyond the province of (mere) men (p. 27; also, pp. 42-43). This is not convincing since no punishment, whether on retributive or deterent grounds, need imply belief in the total evilness of the punishee— all that need be believed (for retribution) is that what the offender has done is as evil as the punishment is awful, or (for deterrence) that what he has done is awful enough to warrant whatever punishment will discourage others from doing it. "Execution," writes van den Haag, "merely presumes an identification [with evil] sufficient to disregard what good qualities the convict has (he may be nice to animals and love his mother).

No total identification with evil—whatever that means—is required; only a "sufficiently wicked crime" (p. 35).

Thus far I have tried to indicate how difficult it is to make an argument for the abolition of the death penalty against which the death penalty advocate cannot successfully defend himself. But van den Haag's argument is not merely defensive—he poses a positive challenge to anyone who would take up the abolitionist cause. For van den Haag, in order to argue convincingly for abolition, one must prove either that "no [criminal] act, however horrible, justifies [that is, deserves] the death penalty," or that, if capital punishment were found to deter murder more effectively than life imprisonment, we should still "prefer to preserve the life of a convicted murderer rather than the lives of innocent victims, even if it were certain that these victims would be spared if the murderer were executed" (p. 275).

If van den Haag is right and the abolitionist cause depends on proving either or both of these assertions, then it is a lost cause, since I believe they cannot be proven for reasons of the following sort: If people ever deserve anything for their acts, then it seems that what they deserve is something commensurate in cost or in benefit to what they have done. However horrible executions are, there are surely some acts to which they are commensurate in cost. If, as Camus says, the condemned man dies two deaths, one on the scaffold and one anticipating it, then isn't execution justified for one who has murdered two people? if not two, then ten?[6] As for the second assertion, since we take as justified the killing of innocent people (say, homicidal maniacs) in self-defense (that is, when necessary to preserve the lives of their innocent victims), then it seems that we must take as justified the killing of *guilty* people if it is necessary to preserve the lives of innocent victims. Indeed, though punishment is not the same as self-defense, it is, when practiced to deter crimes, arguably a form of social defense—and parity of reason would seem to dictate that if killing is justified when necessary for self-defense, then it is justified when necessary for social defense.

It might be thought that injuring or killing others in self-defense is justifiable in that it aims to stop the threatening individual himself but that punishing people (even guilty people) to deter others is a violation of the Kantian prohibition against using people merely as means to the well-being of others.[7] It seems to me that this objection is premised on the belief that what deters potential criminals are the individual acts of punishment. In that case, each person punished is truly being used for the benefit of others. If, however, what deters potential criminals is the existence of a functioning punishment system, then everyone is benefited by that system, including those who end up being punished by it, since they too have received the benefit of enhanced security due to the deterring of some potential criminals. Even criminals benefit from what deters other criminals from preying on them. Then, each act of punishment is done as a necessary condition of the existence of a system that benefits all; and no one is used or sacrificed *merely* for the benefit or others.

If I am correct in believing that the assertions that van den Haag challenges the abolitionist to prove cannot be proven, then the case for the abolition of the death penalty must be made while accepting that some crimes deserve capital punishment, and that evidence that capital punishment was a substantially better deterrent to murder than life imprisonment would justify imposing it. This is what I shall attempt to do. Indeed, I shall begin the case for the abolition of the death penalty by defending the justice of the death penalty as a punishment for murder.

II. JUST DESERTS AND JUST PUNISHMENTS

In my view, the death penalty is a just punishment for murder because the *lex talionis,* an eye for an eye, and so on, is just, although, as I shall suggest at the end of this section, it can only be rightly applied when its implied preconditions are satisfied. The *lex talionis* is a version of retributivism. Retributivism—as the word itself suggests—is the doctrine that the offender should be *paid back* with suffering he deserves because of the evil he has done, and the *lex talionis* asserts that injury equivalent to that he imposed is what the offender deserves.[8] But the *lex talionis* is not the only version of retributivism. Another, which I shall call "proportional retributivism," holds that what retribution requires is not equality of injury between crimes and punishments, but "fit" or proportionality, such that the worst crime is punished with the society's worst penalty, and so on, though the society's worst punishment need not duplicate the injury of the worst crime.[9] Later, I shall try to show how a form of proportional retributivism is compatible with acknowledging the justice of the *lex talionis.* Indeed, since I shall defend the justice of the *lex talionis,* I take such compatibility as a necessary condition of the validity of any form of retributivism.[10]

There is nothing self-evident about the justice of the *lex talionis* nor, for that matter, of retributivism.[11] The standard problem confronting those who would justify retributivism is that of overcoming the suspicion that it does no more than sanctify the victim's desire to hurt the offender back. Since serving that desire amounts to hurting the offender simply for the satisfaction that the victim derives from seeing the offender suffer, and since deriving satisfaction from the suffering of others seems primitive, the policy of imposing suffering on the offender for no other purpose than giving satisfaction to his victim seems primitive as well. Consequently, defending retributivism requires showing that the suffering imposed on the wrongdoer has some worthy point beyond the satisfaction of victims. In what follows, I shall try to identify a proposition—which I call the *retributivist principle*—that I take to be the nerve of retributivism. I think this principle accounts for the justice of the *lex talionis* and indicates the point of the suffering demanded by retributivism. Not to do too much of the work of the death penalty advocate, I shall make no extended argument for this principle beyond suggesting the considerations that make it plausible. I shall identify these considerations by drawing, with considerable license, on Hegel and Kant.

I think that we can see the justice of the *lex talionis* by focusing on the striking affinity between it and the *golden rule*. The *golden rule* mandates "Do unto others as you would have others do unto you," while the *lex talionis* counsels "Do unto others as they have done unto you." It would not be too far-fetched to say that the *lex talionis* is the law enforcement arm of the golden rule, at least in the sense that if people were actually treated as they treated others, then everyone would necessarily follow the golden rule because then people could only willingly act toward others as they were willing to have others act toward them. This is not to suggest that the *lex talionis* follows from the golden rule, but rather that the two share a common moral inspiration: the equality of persons. Treating others as you *would* have them treat you means treating others as equal to you, because adopting the golden rule as one's guiding principle implies that one counts the suffering of others to be as great a calamity as one's own suffering, that one counts one's right to impose suffering on others as no greater than their right to impose suffering on one, and so on. This leads to the *lex talionis* by two approaches that start from different points and converge.

I call the first approach "Hegelian" because Hegel held (roughly) that crime upsets the equality between persons and retributive punishment restores that equality by "annulling" the crime.[12] As we have seen, acting according to the golden rule implies treating others as your equals. Conversely, violating the golden rule implies the reverse: Doing to another what you would *not* have that other do to you violates the equality of persons by asserting a right toward the other that the other does not possess toward you. Doing back to you what you did "annuls" your violation by reasserting that the other has the same right toward you that you assert toward him. Punishment according to the *lex talionis* cannot heal the injury that the other has suffered at your hands, rather it rectifies the indignity he has suffered, by restoring him to equality with you.

"Equality of persons" here does not mean equality of concern for their happiness, as it might for a utilitarian. On such a (roughly) utilitarian understanding of equality, imposing suffering on the wrongdoer equivalent to the suffering he has imposed would have little point. Rather, equality of concern for people's happiness would lead us to impose as little suffering on the wrongdoer as was compatible with maintaining the happiness of others. This is enough to show that retributivism (at least in this "Hegelian" form) reflects a conception of morality quite different from that envisioned by utilitarianism. Instead of seeing morality as administering doses of happiness to individual recipients, the retributivist envisions morality as maintaining the relations appropriate to equally sovereign individuals. A crime, rather than representing a unit of suffering added to the already considerable suffering in the world, is an assault on the sovereignty of an individual that temporarily places one person (the criminal) in a position of illegimate sovereignty over another (the victim). The victim (or his representative, the state) then has the right to rectify this loss of standing relative to the criminal by meting out a punishment that reduces the criminal's sovereignty in the degree to which he vaunted it above his victim's. It might be thought that this is a duty, not just a right, but that is surely too much. The victim has the right to forgive the violator without punishment, which suggests that it is by virtue of having the right to punish the violator (rather than the duty) that the victim's equality with the violator is restored.

I call the second approach "Kantian" since Kant held (roughly) that, since reason (like justice) is no respecter of the sheer difference between individuals, when a rational being decides to act in a certain way toward his fellows, he implicitly authorizes similar action by his fellows toward him.[13] A version of the golden rule, then, is a requirement of reason: acting rationally, one always acts as he would have others act toward him. Consequently, to act toward a person as he has acted toward others is to treat him as a rational being, that is, as if his act were the product of a rational decision. From this, it may be concluded that we have a duty to do to offenders what they have done, since this amounts to according them the respect due rational beings.[14] Here too, however, the assertion of a duty to punish seems excessive, since, if this duty arises because doing to people what they have done to others is necessary to accord them the respect due rational beings, then we would have a duty to do to all rational persons *everything*—good, bad, or indifferent—that they do to others. The point rather is that, by his acts, a rational being *authorizes* others to do the same to him, he doesn't *compel* them to. Here too, then, the argument leads to a right, rather than a duty, to exact the *lex talionis*. And this is supported by the fact that we can conclude from Kant's argument that a rational being cannot validly complain of being treated in the way he has treated others, and where there is no valid complaint, there is no injustice, and where there is no injustice, others have acted within their rights.[15] It should be clear that the Kantian argument also rests on the equality of persons, because a rational agent only implicitly authorizes having done to him action similar to what he has done to another, if he and the other are similar in the relevant ways.

The "Hegelian" and "Kantian" approaches arrive at the same destination from opposite sides. The "Hegelian" approach starts from the victim's equality with the criminal, and infers from it the victim's right to do to the criminal what the criminal has done to the victim. The "Kantian" approach starts from the criminal's rationality, and infers from it the criminal's authorization of the victim's right to do to the criminal what the criminal has done to the victim. Taken together, these approaches support the following proposition: The equality and rationality of persons implies that an offender deserves and his victim has the right to impose suffering on the offender equal to that which he imposed on the victim. This is the proposition I call the *retributivist principle*, and I shall assume henceforth that it is true. This principle provides that the *lex talionis* is the criminal's just desert and the victim's (or as his representative, the state's) right. Moreover, the principle also indicates the point of retributive punishment, namely, it affirms the equality and rationality of persons, victims and offenders alike.[16] And the point of this affirmation is, like any moral affirmation, to make a statement, to the criminal, to impress upon him his equality with his victim (which earns him a like fate) and his rationality (by which his actions are held to authorize his fate), and to the society, so that recognition of the equality and rationality of persons becomes a visible part of our shared moral environment that none can ignore in justifying their actions to one another.

When I say that with respect to the criminal, the point of retributive punishment is to impress upon him his equality with his victim, I mean to be understood quite literally. If the sentence is just and the criminal rational, then the punishment should normally *force* upon him recognition of his equality with his victim, recognition of their shared vulnerability to suffering and their shared desire to avoid it, as well as recognition of the fact that he counts for no more than his victim in the eyes of their fellows. For this reason, the retributivist requires that the offender be sane, not only at the moment of his crime, but also at the moment of his punishment—while this latter requirement would seem largely pointless (if not downright malevolent) to a utilitarian. Incidentally, it is, I believe, the desire that the offender be forced by suffering punishment to recognize his equality with his victim, rather than the desire for that suffering itself, that constitutes what is rational in the desire for revenge.

The retributivist principle represents a conception of moral desert whose complete elaboration would take us far beyond the scope of the present essay. In its defense, however, it is worth noting that our common notion of moral desert seems to include (at least) two elements: (1) a conception of individual responsibility for actions that is "contagious," that is, one which confers moral justification on the punishing (or rewarding) reactions of others; and (2) a measure of the relevant worth of actions that determines the legitimate magnitude of justified reactions. Broadly speaking, the "Kantian" notion of authorization implicit in rational action supplies the first element, and the "Hegelian" notion of upsetting and restoring equality of standing supplies the second. It seems, then, reasonable to take the equality and rationality of persons as implying moral desert in the way asserted in the retributivist principle. I shall assume henceforth that the retributivist principle is true.

The truth of the retributivist principle establishes the justice of the *lex talionis*, but, since it establishes this as a right of the victim rather than a duty, it does not settle the question of whether or to what extent the victim or the state should exercise this right and exact the *lex talionis*. This is a separate moral question because strict adherence to the *lex talionis* amounts to allowing criminals, even the most barbaric of them, to dictate our punishing behavior. It seems certain that there are at least some crimes, such as rape or torture, that we ought not try to match. And this is not merely a matter of imposing an alternative punishment that produces an equivalent amount of suffering, as, say, some number of years in prison that might "add up" to the harm caused by a rapist or a torturer. Even if no amount of time in prison would add up to the harm caused by a torturer, it still seems that we ought not torture him even if this were the only way of making him suffer as much as he has made his victim suffer. Or, consider someone who has committed several murders in cold blood. On the *lex talionis,* it would seem that such a criminal might justly be brought to within an inch of death and then revived (or to within a moment of execution and then reprieved) as many times as he has killed (minus one), and then finally executed. But surely this is a degree of cruelty that would be monstrous.[17]

Since the retributivist principle establishes the *lex talionis* as the victim's right, it might seem that the question of how far this right should be exercised is "up to the victim." And indeed, this would be the case in the state of nature. But once, for all the good reasons familiar to readers of John Locke, the state comes into existence, public punishment replaces private, and the victim's right to punish reposes in the state. With this, the decision as to how far to exercise this right goes to the state as well. To be sure, since (at least with respect to retributive punishment) the victim's right is the source of the state's right to punish, the state must exercise its right in ways that are faithful to the victim's right. Later, when I try to spell out the upper and lower limits of just punishment, these may be taken as indicating the range within which the state can punish and remain faithful to the victim's right.

I suspect that it will be widely agreed that the state ought not administer punishments of the sort described above even if required by the letter of the *lex talionis,* and thus, even granting the justice of *lex talionis,* there are occasions on which it is morally appropriate to diverge from its requirements. We must, of course, distinguish such morally based divergence from that which is based on practicality. Like any moral principle, the *lex talionis* is subject to "ought implies can." It will usually be impossible to do to an offender exactly what he has done—for example, his offense will normally have had an element of surprise that is not possible for a judicially imposed punishment, but this fact can hardly free him from having to bear the suffering he has imposed on another. Thus, for reasons of practicality, the *lex talionis* must necessarily be qualified to call for doing to the offender *as nearly as possible* what he has done to his victim. When, however, we refrain from raping rapists or torturing torturers, we do so for reasons of morality, not of practicality. And, given the justice of the *lex talionis,* these moral reasons cannot amount to claiming that it would be *unjust* to rape rapists or torture torturers. Rather the claim must be that, even though it would be just to rape rapists and torture torturers, other moral considerations weigh against doing so.

On the other hand, when, for moral reasons, we refrain from exacting the *lex talionis,* and impose a less harsh alternative punishment, it may be said that we are not doing full justice to the criminal, but it cannot automatically be the case that we are doing an *injustice* to his victim. Otherwise we would have to say it was unjust to imprison our torturer rather than torturing him or to simply execute our multiple murderer rather than multiply "executing" him. Surely it is counterintuitive (and irrational to boot) to set the demands of justice so high that a society would have to choose between being barbaric or being unjust. This would effectively price justice out of the moral market.

The implication of this is that there is a range of just punishments that includes some that are just though they exact less than the full measure of the *lex talionis.* What are the top and bottom ends of this range? I think that both are indicated by the *retributivist principle.* The principle identifies the *lex talionis* as the offender's desert and since, on retributive grounds, punishment beyond what one deserves is unjust for the same reasons that make punishment of the innocent unjust, the *lex talionis* is the upper limit of the range of just punishments. On the other hand, if the retributivist principle is true, then denying that the offender deserves suffering equal to that which he imposed amounts to denying the equality and rationality of persons. From this it follows that we fall below the bottom end of the range of just punishments when we act in ways that are incompatible with the *lex talionis* at the top end. That is, we fall below the bottom end and commit an injustice to the victim when we treat the offender in a way that is no longer compatible with sincerely believing that he deserves to have done to him what he has done to his victim. Thus, the upper limit of the range of just punishments is the point after which more punishment is unjust to the offender, and the lower limit is the point after which less punishment is unjust to the victim. In this way, the range of just punishments remains faithful to the victim's right which is their source.

This way of understanding just punishment enables us to formulate proportional retributivism so that it is compatible with acknowledging the justice of the *lex talionis:* If we take the *lex talionis* as spelling out the offender's just deserts, and if other moral considerations require us to refrain from matching the injury caused by the offender while still allowing us to punish justly, then surely we impose just punishment if we impose the closest morally acceptable approximation to the *lex talionis*. Proportional retributivism, then, in requiring that the worst crime be punished by the society's worst punishment and so on, could be understood as translating the offender's just desert into its nearest equivalent in the society's table of morally acceptable punishments. Then the two versions of retributivism (*lex talionis* and proportional) are related in that the first states what just punishment would be if nothing but the offender's just desert mattered, and the second locates just punishment at the meeting point of the offender's just deserts and the society's moral scruples. And since this second version only modifies the requirements of the *lex talionis* in light of other moral considerations, it is compatible with believing that the *lex talionis* spells out the offender's just deserts, much in the way that modifying the obligations of promisers in light of other moral considerations is compatible with believing in the binding nature of promises.

Proportional retributivism so formulated preserves the point of retributivism and remains faithful to the victim's right which is its source. Since it punishes with the closest morally acceptable approximation to the *lex talionis,* it effectively says to the offender, you deserve the equivalent of what you did to your victim and you are getting less only to the degree that *our* moral scruples limit us from duplicating what you have done. Such punishment, then, affirms the equality of persons by respecting *as far as is morally permissible* the victim's right to impose suffering on the offender equal to what he received, and it affirms the rationality of the offender by treating him as authorizing others to do to him what he has done though they take him up on it only *as far as is morally permissible.* Needless to say, the alternative punishments must in some convincing ways be comparable in gravity to the crimes which they punish, or else they will trivialize the harms those crimes caused and be no longer compatible with sincerely believing that the offender deserves to have done to him what he has done to his victim and no longer capable of impressing upon the criminal his equality with the victim. If we punish rapists with a small fine or a brief prison term, we do an injustice to their victims, because this trivializes the suffering rapists have caused and thus is incompatible with believing that they deserve to have done to them something comparable to what they have done to their victims. If, on the other hand, instead of raping rapists we impose on them some grave penalty, say a substantial term of imprisonment, then we do no injustice even though we refrain from exacting the *lex talionis.*

To sum up, I take the *lex talionis* to be the top end of the range of just punishments. When, because we are simply unable to duplicate the criminal's offense, we modify the *lex talionis* subject to call for imposing on the offender as nearly as possible what he has done, we are still at this top end, applying the *lex talionis* subject to "ought implies can." When we do less than this, we still act justly as long as we punish in a way that is compatible with sincerely believing that the offender deserves the full measure of the *lex talionis,* but receives less for reasons that do not undermine this belief. If this is true, then it is not unjust to spare murderers as long as they can be punished in some other suitably grave way. I leave open the question of what such an alternative punishment might be, except to say that it need not be limited to such penalties as are currently imposed. For example, though rarely carried out in practice, a life sentence with no chance of parole might be a civilized equivalent of the death penalty—after all, people sentenced to life imprisonment have traditionally been regarded as "civilly dead."[18]

It might be objected that no punishment short of death will serve the point of retributivism with respect to murderers because no punishment short of death is commensurate with the crime of murder since, while some number of years of imprisonment may add up to the amount of harm done by rapists or assaulters or torturers, no number of years will add up to the harm done to the victim of murder. But justified divergence from the *lex talionis* is not limited only to changing the form of punishment while maintaining equivalent severity. Otherwise, we would have to torture torturers rather than imprison them if they tortured more than could be made up for by years in prison (or by the years available to them to spend in prison, which might be few for elderly torturers), and we would have to subject multiple murderers to multiple "executions." If justice allows us to refrain from these penalties, then justice allows punishments that are not equal in suffering to their crimes. It seems to me that if the objector grants this much, then he must show that a punishment less than death is not merely incommensurate to the harm caused by murder, but so far out of proportion to that harm that it trivializes it and thus effectively denies the equality and rationality of persons. Now, I am vulnerable to the claim that a sentence of life in prison that allows parole after eight or ten years does indeed trivialize the harm of (premeditated, coldblooded) murder. But I cannot see how a sentence that would require a murderer to spend his full natural life in prison, or even the lion's share of his adult life (say, the thirty years between age twenty and age fifty), can be regarded as anything less than extremely severe and thus no trivialization of the harm he has caused.

I take it then that the justice of the *lex talionis* implies that it is just to execute murderers, but not that it is unjust to spare them as long as they are systematically punished in some other suitably grave way. Before developing the implications of this claim, a word about the implied preconditions of applying the *lex talionis* is in order.

Since this principle calls for imposing on offenders the harms they are responsible for imposing on others, the implied preconditions of applying it to any particular harm include the requirement that the harm be one that the offender is fully responsible for, where responsibility is both psychological, the capacity to tell the difference between right and wrong and control one's actions, and social. If people are subjected to remediable unjust social circumstances beyond their control, and if harmful actions are a predictable response to those conditions, then those who benefit from the unjust conditions and refuse to remedy them share responsibility for the harmful acts—and thus neither their doing nor their cost can be assigned fully to the offenders alone. For example, if a slave kills an innocent person while making his escape, at least part of the blame for the killing must fall on those who have enslaved him. And this is because slavery is unjust, not merely because the desire to escape from slavery is understandable. The desire to escape from prison is understandable as well, but if the imprisonment were a just sentence, then we would hold the prisoner, and not his keepers, responsible if he killed someone while escaping.

Since I believe that the vast majority of murders in America are a predictable response to the frustrations and disabilities of impoverished social circumstances,[19] and since I believe that that impoverishment is a remediable injustice from which others in America benefit, I believe that we have no right to exact the full cost of murders from our murderers until we have done everything possible to rectify the conditions that produce their crimes.[20] But these are the "Reagan years," and not many—who are not already susceptible—will be persuaded by this sort of argument.[21] This does not, in my view, shake its validity; but I want to make an argument whose appeal is not limited to those who think that crime is the result of social injustice.[22] I shall proceed then, granting not only the justice of the death penalty, but also, at least temporarily, the assumption that our murderers are wholly deserving of dying for their crimes. If I can show that it would still be wrong to execute murderers, I believe I shall have made the strongest case for abolishing the death penalty.

III. CIVILIZATION, PAIN, AND JUSTICE

As I have already suggested, from the fact that something is justly deserved, it does not automatically follow that it should be done, since there may be other moral reasons for not doing it such that, all told, the weight of moral reasons swings the balance against proceeding. The same argument that I have given for the justice of the death penalty for murderers proves the justice of beating assaulters, raping rapists, and torturing torturers. Nonetheless, I believe, and suspect that most would agree, that it would not be right for us to beat assaulters, rape rapists, or torture torturers, *even though it were their just deserts*—and even if this were the only way to make them suffer as much as they had made their victims suffer. Calling for the abolition of the death penalty, though it be just, then, amounts to urging that as a society we place execution in the same category of sanction as beating, raping, and torturing, and treat it as something it would also not be right for us to do to offenders, *even if it were their just deserts.*

To argue for placing execution in this category, I must show what would be gained therefrom; and to show that, I shall indicate what we gain from placing torture in this category and argue that a similar gain is to be had from doing the same with execution. I select torture because I think the reasons for placing it in this category are, due to the extremity of torture, most easily seen—but what I say here applies with appropriate modification to other severe physical punishments, such as beating and raping. First, and most evidently, placing torture in this category broadcasts the message that we as a society judge torturing so horrible a thing to do to a person that we refuse to do it even when it is deserved. Note that such a judgment does not commit us to an absolute prohibition on torturing. No matter how horrible we judge something to be, we may still be justified in doing it if it is necessary to prevent something even worse. Leaving this aside for the moment, what is gained by broadcasting the public judgment that torture is too horrible to inflict even if deserved?

I think the answer to this lies in what we understand as civilization. In *The Genealogy of Morals,* Nietzsche says that in early times "pain did not hurt as much as it does today."[23] The truth in this puzzling remark is that progress in civilization is characterized by a lower tolerance for one's own pain and that suffered by others. And this is appropriate, since, via growth in knowledge, civilization brings increased power to prevent or reduce pain and, via growth in the ability to communicate and interact with more and more people, civilization extends the circle of people with whom we empathize.[24] If civilization is characterized by lower tolerance for our own pain and that of others, then publicly refusing to do horrible things to our fellows both signals the level of our civilization *and, by our example, continues the work of civilizing.* And this gesture is all the more powerful if we refuse to do horrible things to those who deserve them. I contend then that the more things we are able to include in this category, the more civilized we are and the more civili*zing.* Thus we gain from including torture in this category, and if execution is especially horrible, we gain still more by including it.

Needless to say, the content, direction, and even the worth of civilization are hotly contested issues, and I shall not be able to win those contests in this brief space. At a minimum, however, I shall assume that civilization involves the taming of the natural environment and of the human animals in it, and that the overall trend in human history is toward increasing this taming, though the trend is by no means unbroken or without reverses. On these grounds, we can say that growth in civilization generally marks human history, that a reduction in the horrible things we tolerate doing to our fellows (even when they deserve them) is part of this growth, and that once the work of civilization is taken on consciously, it includes carrying forward and expanding this reduction.

This claim broadly corresponds to what Emile Durkheim identified, nearly a century ago, as "two laws which seem . . . to prevail in the evolution of the apparatus of punishment." The first, the law of quantitative change, Durkheim formulates as:

> The intensity of punishment is the greater the more closely societies approximate to a less developed type—and the more the central power assumes an absolute character.

And the second, which Durkheim refers to as the law of qualitative change, is:

> Deprivations of liberty, and of liberty alone, varying in time according to the seriousness of the crime, tend to become more and more the normal means of social control.[25]

Several things should be noted about these laws. First of all, they are not two separate laws. As Durkheim understands them, the second exemplifies the trend toward moderation of punishment referred to in the first.[26] Second, the first law really refers to two distinct trends, which usually coincide but do not always. That is, moderation of punishment accompanies *both* the movement from less to more advanced types of society *and* the movement from more to less absolute rule. Normally these go hand in hand, but where they do not, the effect of one trend may offset the effect of the other. Thus, a primitive society without absolute rule may have milder punishments than an equally primitive but more absolutist society.[27] This complication need not trouble us, since the claim I am making refers to the first trend, namely, that punishments tend to become milder as societies become more advanced; and that this is a trend in history is not refuted by the fact that it is accompanied by other trends and even occasionally offset by them. Moreover, I shall close this article with a suggestion about the relation between the intensity of punishment and the justice of society, which might broadly be thought of as corresponding to the second trend in Durkheim's first law. Finally, and most important for our purposes, is the fact that Durkheim's claim that punishment becomes less intense as societies become more advanced is a generalization that he supports with an impressive array of evidence from historical societies from pre-Christian times to the time in which he wrote—and this in turn supports my claim that the reduction in the horrible things we do to our fellows is in fact part of the advance of civilization.[28]

Against this it might be argued that many things grow in history, some good, some bad, and some mixed, and thus the fact that there is some historical trend is not a sufficient reason to continue it. Thus, for example, history also brings growth in population, but we are not for that reason called upon to continue the work of civilization by continually increasing our population. What this suggests is that in order to identify something as part of the work of civilizing, we must show not only that it generally grows in history, but that its growth is, on some independent grounds, clearly an advance for the human species—that is, either an unmitigated gain or at least consistently a net gain. And this implies that even trends which we might generally regard as advances may in some cases bring losses with them, such that when they did it would not be appropriate for us to lend our efforts to continuing them. Of such trends we can say that they are advances in civilization except when their gains are outweighed by the losses they bring—and that we are only called upon to further these trends when their gains are *not* outweighed in this way. It is clear in this light that increasing population is a mixed blessing at best, bringing both gains and losses. Consequently, it is not always an advance in civilization that we should further, though at times it may be.

What can be said of reducing the horrible things that we do to our fellows even when deserved? First of all, given our vulnerability to pain, it seems clearly a gain. Is it however an unmitigated gain? That is, would such a reduction ever amount to a loss? It seems to me that there are two conditions under which it would be a loss, namely, if the reduction made our lives more dangerous, or if not doing what is justly deserved were a loss in itself. Let us leave aside the former, since, as I have already suggested and as I will soon indicate in greater detail, I accept that if some horrible punishment is necessary to deter equally or more horrible acts, then we may have to impose the punishment. Thus my claim is that reduction in the horrible things we do to our fellows is an advance in civilization *as long as our lives are not thereby made more dangerous,* and that it is only then that we are called upon to extend that reduction as part of the work of civilization. Assuming then, for the moment, that we suffer no increased danger by refraining from doing horrible things to our fellows when they justly deserve them, does such refraining to do what is justly deserved amount to a loss?

It seems to me that the answer to this must be that refraining to do what is justly deserved is only a loss where it amounts to doing an injustice. But such refraining to do what is just is not doing what is unjust, unless what we do instead falls below the bottom end of the range of just punishments. Otherwise, it would be unjust to refrain from torturing torturers, raping rapists, or beating assaulters. In short, I take it that if there is no injustice in refraining from torturing torturers, then there is no injustice in refraining to do horrible things to our fellows generally, when they deserve them, as long as what we do instead is compatible with believing that they do deserve them. And thus that if such refraining does not make our lives more dangerous, then it is no loss, and given our vulnerability to pain, it is a gain. Consequently, reduction in the horrible things we do to our fellows, when not necessary to our protection, is an advance in civilization that we are called upon to continue once we consciously take upon ourselves the work of civilization.

To complete the argument, however, I must show that execution is horrible enough to warrant its inclusion alongside torture. Against this it will be said that execution is not especially horrible since it only hastens a fate that is inevitable for us.[29] I think that this view overlooks important differences in the manner in which people reach their inevitable ends. I contend that execution is especially horrible, and it is so in a way similar to (though not identical with) the way in which torture is especially horrible. I believe we view torture as especially awful because of two of its features, which also characterize execution: intense pain and the spectacle of one human being completely subject to the power of another. This latter is separate from the issue of pain since it is something that offends us about unpainful things, such as slavery (even voluntarily entered) and prostitution (even voluntarily chosen as an occupation).[30] Execution shares this separate feature, since killing a bound and defenseless human being enacts the total subjugation of that person to his fellows. I think, incidentally, that this accounts for the general uneasiness with which execution by lethal injection has been greeted. Rather than humanizing the event, it seems only to have purchased a possible reduction in physical pain at the price of increasing the spectacle of subjugation—with no net gain in the attractiveness of the death penalty. Indeed, its net effect may have been the reverse.

In addition to the spectacle of subjugation, execution, even by physically painless means, is also characterized by a special and intense psychological pain that distinguishes it from the loss of life that awaits us all. Interesting in this regard is the fact that although we are not terribly squeamish about the loss of life itself, allowing it in war, self-defense, as a necessary cost of progress, and so on, we are, as the extraordinary hesitance of our courts testifies, quite reluctant to execute. I think this is because execution involves the most psychologically painful features of deaths. We normally regard death from human causes as worse than death from natural causes, since a humanly caused shortening of life lacks the consolation of unavoidability. And we normally regard death whose coming is foreseen by its victim as worse than sudden death, because a foreseen death adds to the loss of life the terrible consciousness of that impending loss.[31] As a humanly caused death whose advent is foreseen by its victim, an execution combines the worst of both.

Thus far, by analogy with torture, I have argued that execution should be avoided because of how horrible it is to the one executed. But there are reasons of another sort that follow from the analogy with torture. Torture is to be avoided not only because of what it says about *what* we are willing to do to our fellows, but also because of what it says about *us* who are willing to do it. To torture someone is an awful spectacle not only because of the intensity of pain imposed, but because of what is required to be able to impose such pain on one's fellows. The tortured body cringes, using its full exertion to escape the pain imposed upon it—it literally begs for relief with its muscles as it does with its cries. To torture someone is to demonstrate a capacity to resist this begging, and that in turn demonstrates a kind of hardheartedness that a society ought not parade.

And this is true not only of torture, but of all severe corporal punishment. Indeed, I think this constitutes part of the answer to the puzzling question of why we refrain from punishments like whipping, even when the alternative (some months in jail versus some lashes) seems more costly to the offender. Imprisonment is painful to be sure, but it is a reflective pain, one that comes with comparing what is to what might have been, and that can be temporarily ignored by thinking about other things. But physical pain has an urgency that holds body and mind in a fierce grip. Of physical pain, as Orwell's Winston Smith recognized, "you could only wish one thing: that it should stop."[32] Refraining from torture in particular and corporal punishment in general, we both refuse to put a fellow human being in this grip *and* refuse to show our ability to resist this wish. The death penalty is the last corporal punishment used officially in the modern world. And it is corporal not only because administered via the body, but because the pain of foreseen, humanly administered death strikes us with the urgency that characterizes intense physical pain, causing grown men to cry, faint, and lose control of their bodily functions. There is something to be gained by refusing to endorse the hardness of heart necessary to impose such a fate.

By placing execution alongside torture in the category of things we will not do to our fellow human beings even when they deserve them, we broadcast the message that totally subjugating a person to the power of others *and* confronting him with the advent of his own humanly administered demise is too horrible to be done by civilized human beings to their fellows even when they have earned it: too horrible to do, and too horrible to be capable of doing. And I contend that broadcasting this message loud and clear would in the long run contribute to the general detestation of murder and be, to the extent to which it worked itself into the hearts and minds of the populace, a deterrent. In short, refusing to execute murderers though they deserve it both reflects and continues the taming of the human species that we call civilization. Thus, I take it that the abolition of the death penalty, though it is a just punishment for murder, is part of the civilizing mission of modern states.

IV. CIVILIZATION, SAFETY, AND DETERRENCE

Earlier I said that judging a practice too horrible to do even to those who deserve it does not exclude the possibility that it could be justified if necessary to avoid even worse consequences. Thus, were the death penalty clearly proven a better deterrent to the murder of innocent people than life in prison, we might have to admit that we had not yet reached a level of civilization at which we could protect ourselves without imposing this horrible fate on murderers, and thus we might have to grant the necessity of instituting the death penalty.[33] But this is far from proven. The available research by no means clearly indicates that the death penalty reduces the incidence of homicide more than life imprisonment does. Even the econometric studies of Isaac Ehrlich, which purport to show that each execution saves seven or eight potential murder victims, have not changed this fact, as is testified to by the controversy and objections from equally respected statisticians that Ehrlich's work has provoked.[34]

Conceding that it has not been proven that the death penalty deters more murders than life imprisonment, van den Haag has argued that neither has it been proven that the death penalty does *not* deter more murders,[35] and thus we must follow common sense which teaches that the higher the cost of something, the fewer people will choose it, and therefore at least some potential murderers who would not be deterred by life imprisonment will be deterred by the death penalty. Van den Haag writes:

> . . . our experience shows that the greater the threatened penalty, the more it deters.
> . . . Life in prison is still life, however unpleasant. In contrast, the death penalty does not just threaten to make life unpleasant—it threatens to take life altogether. This difference is perceived by those affected. We find that when they have the choice between life in prison and execution, 99% of all prisoners under sentence of death prefer life in prison. . . .
> From this unquestioned fact a reasonable conclusion can be drawn in favor of the superior deterrent effect of the death penalty. Those who have the choice in practice . . . fear death more than they fear life in prison. . . . If they do, it follows that the threat of the death penalty, all other things equal, is likely to deter more than the threat of life in prison. One is most deterred by what one fears most. From which it follows that whatever statistics fail, or do not fail, to show, the death penalty is likely to be more deterrent than any other. [Pp. 68-69][36]

Those of us who recognize how common-sensical it was, and still is, to believe that the sun moves around the earth, will be less willing than Professor van den Haag to follow common sense here, especially when it comes to doing something awful to our fellows. Moreover, there are good reasons for doubting common sense on this matter. Here are four:

1. From the fact that one penalty is more feared than another, it does not follow that the more feared penalty will deter more than the less feared, unless we know that the less feared penalty is not fearful enough to deter everyone who can be deterred—and this is just what we don't know with regard to the death penalty. Though I fear the death penalty more than life in prison, I can't think of any act that the death penalty would deter me from that an equal likelihood of spending my life in prison wouldn't deter me from as well.[37] Since it seems to me that whoever would be deterred by a given likelihood of death would be deterred by an *equal* likelihood of life behind bars, I suspect that the common-sense argument only seems plausible because we evaluate it unconsciously assuming that potential criminals will face larger likelihoods of death sentences than of life sentences. If the likelihoods were equal, it seems to me that where life imprisonment was improbable enough to make it too distant a possibility to worry much about, a similar low probability of death would have the same effect. After

all, we are undeterred by small likelihoods of death every time we walk the streets. And if life imprisonment were sufficiently probable to pose a real deterrent threat, it would pose as much of a deterrent threat as death. And this is just what most of the research we have on the comparative deterrent impact of execution versus life imprisonment suggests.

2. In light of the fact that roughly 500 to 700 suspected felons are killed by the police in the line of duty every year, and the fact that the number of privately owned guns in America is substantially larger than the number of households in America, it must be granted that anyone contemplating committing a crime *already* faces a substantial risk of ending up dead as a result.[38] It's hard to see why anyone *who is not already deterred by this* would be deterred by the addition of the more distant risk of death after apprehension, conviction, and appeal. Indeed, this suggests that people consider risks in a much cruder way than van den Haag's appeal to common sense suggests—which should be evident to anyone who contemplates how few people use seatbelts (14% of drivers, on some estimates), when it is widely known that wearing them can spell the difference between life (outside prison) and death.[39]

3. Van den Haag has maintained that deterrence doesn't work only by means of cost-benefit calculations made by potential criminals. It works also by the lesson about the wrongfulness of murder that is slowly learned in a society that subjects murderers to the ultimate punishment (p. 63). But if I am correct in claiming that the refusal to execute even those who deserve it has a civilizing effect, then the refusal to execute also teaches a lesson about the wrongfulness of murder. My claim here is admittedly speculative, but no more so than van den Haag's to the contrary. And my view has the added virtue of accounting for the failure of research to show an increased deterrent effect from executions *without having to deny the plausibility of van den Haag's common-sense argument that at least some additional potential murderers will be deterred by the prospect of the death penalty.* If there is a deterrent effect from *not executing,* then it is understandable that while executions will deter some murderers, this effect will be balanced out by the weakening of the deterrent effect of not executing, such that no net reduction in murders will result.[40] And this, by the way, also disposes of van den Haag's argument that, in the absence of knowledge one way or the other on the deterrent effect of executions, we should execute murderers rather than risk the lives of innocent people whose murders might have been deterred if we had. If there is a deterrent effect of not executing, it follows that we risk innocent lives either way. And if this is so, it seems that the only reasonable course of action is to refrain from imposing what we know is a horrible fate.[41]

4. Those who still think that van den Haag's common-sense argument for executing murderers is valid will find that the argument proves more

than they bargained for. Van den Haag maintains that, in the absence of conclusive evidence on the relative deterrent impact of the death penalty versus life imprisonment, we must follow common sense and assume that if one punishment is more fearful than another, it will deter some potential criminals not deterred by the less fearful punishment. Since people sentenced to death will almost universally try to get their sentences changed to life in prison, it follows that death is more fearful than life imprisonment, and thus that it will deter some additional murderers. Consequently, we should institute the death penalty to save the lives these additional murderers would have taken. But, since people sentenced to be tortured to death would surely try to get their sentences changed to simple execution, the same argument proves that death-by-torture will deter still more potential murderers. Consequently, we should institute death-by-torture to save the lives these additional murderers would have taken. Anyone who accepts van den Haag's argument is then confronted with a dilemma: Until we have conclusive evidence that capital punishment is a greater deterrent to murder than life imprisonment, he must grant *either* that we should not follow common sense and not impose the death penalty; *or* we should follow common sense and torture murderers to death. In short, either we must abolish the electric chair or reinstitute the rack. Surely, this is the *reductio ad absurdum* of van den Haag's common-sense argument.

CONCLUSION: HISTORY, FORCE, AND JUSTICE

I believe that, taken together, these arguments prove that we should abolish the death penalty though it is a just punishment for murder. Let me close with an argument of a different sort. When you see the lash fall upon the backs of Roman slaves, or the hideous tortures meted out in the period of the absolute monarchs, you see more than mere cruelty at work. Surely you suspect that there is something about the injustice of imperial slavery and royal tyranny that requires the use of extreme force to keep these institutions in place. That is, for reasons undoubtedly related to those that support the second part of Durkheims' first law of penal evolution, we take the amount of force a society uses against its own people as an inverse measure of its justness. And though no more than a rough measure, it is a revealing one nonetheless, because when a society is limited in the degree of force it can use against its subjects, it is likely to have to be a juster society since it will have to gain its subjects' cooperation by offering them fairer terms than it would have to, if it could use more force. From this we cannot simply conclude that reducing the force used by our society will automatically make our society more just—but I think we can conclude that it will have this tendency, since it will require us to find means other than force for encouraging compliance with our institutions, and this is likely to require us to make those institutions as fair to all as possible. Thus I hope that America will pose itself the challenge of winning its citizens' cooperation by justice rather than force, and that when future historians look back on the twentieth century, they will find us with countries like France and England and Sweden that have abolished the death penalty, rather than with those like South Africa and the Soviet Union and Iran that have retained it—with all that this suggests about the countries involved.

NOTES

This paper is an expanded version of my opening statement in a debate with Ernest van den Haag on the death penalty at an Amnesty International conference on capital punishment, held at John Jay College in New York City, on October 17, 1983. I am grateful to the Editors of *Philosophy & Public Affairs* for very thought-provoking comments, to Hugo Bedau and Robert Johnson for many helpful suggestions, and to Ernest van den Haag for his encouragement.

1. Asked, in a 1981 Gallup Poll, "Are you in favor of the death penalty for persons convicted of murder?" 66.25% were in favor, 25% were opposed, and 8.75% had no opinion. Asked the same question in 1966, 47.5% were opposed, 41.25% were in favor, and 11.25% had no opinion (Timothy J. Flanagan, David J. van Alstyne, and Michael R. Gottfredson, eds., *Sourcebook of Criminal Justice Statistics—1981*, U.S. Department of Justice, Bureau of Justice Statistics [Washington, D.C.: U.S. Government Printing Office, 1982], p. 209).

2. Ernest van den Haag and John P. Conrad, *The Death Penalty: A Debate* (New York: Plenum Press, 1983). Unless otherwise indicated, page references in the text and notes are to this book.

3. Some days after the first attempt to execute J. D. Autry by lethal injection was aborted, an editorial in *The Washington Post* (14 October 1983) asked: "If the taking of a human life is the most unacceptable of crimes, can it ever be an acceptable penalty? Does an act committed by an individual lose its essential character when it is imposed by society?" (p. A26).

4. "Does fining a criminal show want of respect for property, or imprisoning him, for personal freedom? Just as unreasonable is it to think that to take the life of a man who has taken that of another is to show want of regard for human life. We show, on the contrary, most emphatically our regard for it, by the adoption of a rule that he who violates that right in another forfeits it for himself. . . ." (John Stuart Mill, "Parliamentary Debate on Capital Punishment Within Prisons Bill," in *Philosophical Perspectives on Punishment*, ed. Gertrude Ezorsky [Albany: State University of New York Press, 1972], p. 276; Mill made the speech in 1868.)

5. Mill argues that the possibility of executing an innocent person would be an "invincible" objection "where the mode of criminal procedure is dangerous to the innocent," such as it is "in some parts of the Continent of Europe. . . . But we all know that the defects of our [English] procedure are the very opposite.

Our rules of evidence are even too favorable to the prisoner" (ibid., pp. 276-77).

6. "As a general rule, a man is undone by waiting for capital punishment well before he dies. Two deaths are inflicted on him, the first being worse than the second, whereas he killed but once" (Albert Camus, "Reflections on the Guillotine," in *Resistance, Rebellion and Death* [New York: Alfred A. Knopf, 1969], p. 205). Based on interviews with the condemned men on Alabama's death row, Robert Johnson presents convincing empirical support for Camus' observation, in *Condemned to Life: Life Under Sentence of Death* (New York: Elsevier, 1981).

7. Jeffrie G. Murphy, "Marxism and Retribution," *Philosophy & Public Affairs* 2, no. 3 (Spring 1973):219.

8. I shall speak throughout of retribution as paying back for "harm caused," but this is shorthand for "harm intentionally attempted or caused"; likewise when I speak of the death penalty as punishment for murder, I have in mind premeditated, first-degree murder. Note also that the harm caused by the offender, for which he is to be paid back, is not necessarily limited to the harm done to his immediate victim. It may include as well the suffering of the victim's relatives or the fear produced in the general populace, and the like. For simplicity's sake, however, I shall continue to speak as if the harm for which retributivism would have us pay the offender back is the harm (intentionally attempted or done) to his immediate victim. Also, retribution is not to be confused with *restitution*. Restitution involves restoring the *status quo ante,* the condition prior to the offense. Since it was in this condition that the criminal's offense was committed, it is this condition that constitutes the baseline against which retribution is exacted. Thus retribution involves imposing a loss on the offender measured from the status quo ante. For example, returning a thief's loot to his victim so that the thief and victim now own what they did before the offense is *restitution*. Taking enough from the thief so that what he is left with is less than what he had before the offense is *retribution,* since this is just what he did to his victim.

9. "The most extreme form of retributivism is the law of retaliation: 'an eye for an eye'" (Stanley I. Benn, "Punishment," *The Encyclopedia of Philosophy* 7, ed. Paul Edwards [New York: Macmillan, 1967], p. 32). Hugo Bedau writes: "retributive justice need not be thought to consist of *lex talionis.* One may reject that principle as too crude and still embrace the retributive principle that the severity of punishments should be graded according to the gravity of the offense" (Hugo Bedau, "Capital Punishment," in *Matters of Life and Death,* ed. Tom Regan [New York: Random House, 1980], p. 177). See also, Andrew von Hirsch, "Doing Justice: The Principle of Commensurate Deserts," and Hyman Gross, "Proportional Punishment and Justifiable Sentences," in *Sentencing,* eds. H. Gross and A. von Hirsch (New York: Oxford University Press, 1981), pp. 243-56 and 272-83, respectively. -

10. In an article aimed at defending a retributivist theory of punishment, Michael Davis claims that the relevant measure of punishment is not the cost to the offender's victim ("property taken, bones broken, or lives lost"), but the "value of the unfair advantage he [the offender] takes of those who obey the law (even though they are tempted to do otherwise)" (Michael Davis, "How to Make the Punishment Fit the Crime," *Ethics* 93 [July 1983]:744). Though there is much to be said for

this view, standing alone it seems quite questionable. For example, it would seem that the value of the unfair advantage taken of law-obeyers by one who robs a great deal of money is greater than the value of the unfair advantage taken by a murderer, since the latter gets only the advantage of ridding his world of a nuisance while the former will be able to make a new life without the nuisance and have money left over for other things. This leads to the counterintuitive conclusion that such robbers should be punished more severely (and regarded as more wicked) than murderers. One might try to get around this by treating the value of the unfair advantage as a function of the cost imposed by the crime. And Davis does this after a fashion. He takes the value of such advantages to be equivalent to the prices that licenses to commit crimes would bring if sold on the market, and he claims that these prices would be at least as much as what non-licenseholders would (for their own protection) pay licensees not to use their licenses. Now this obviously brings the cost to victims of crime back into the measure of punishment, though only halfheartedly, since this cost must be added to the value to the licensee of being able to use his license. And this still leaves open the distinct possibility that licenses for very lucrative theft opportunities would fetch higher prices on the market than licenses to kill, with the same counterintuitive result mentioned earlier.

11. Stanley Benn writes: "to say 'it is fitting' or 'justice demands' that the guilty should suffer is only to affirm that punishment is right, not to give grounds for thinking so" (Benn, "Punishment," p. 30).

12. Hegel writes that "The sole positive existence which the injury [i.e., the crime] possesses is that it is the particular will of the criminal [i.e., it is the criminal's intention that distinguishes criminal injury from, say, injury due to an accident]. Hence to injure (or penalize) this particular will as a will determinately existent is to annul the crime, which otherwise would have been held valid, and to restore the right" (G. W. F. Hegel, *The Philosophy of Right,* trans. by T. M. Knox [Oxford: Clarendon Press, 1962; originally published in German in 1821], p. 69, see also p. 331n). I take this to mean that the right is a certain equality of sovereignty between the wills of individuals, crime disrupts that equality by placing one will above others, and punishment restores the equality by annulling the illegitimate ascendance. On these grounds, as I shall suggest below, the desire for revenge (strictly limited to the desire "to even the score") is more respectable than philosophers have generally allowed. And so Hegel writes that "The annulling of crime in this sphere where right is immediate [i.e., the condition prior to conscious morality] is principally revenge, which is just in its content in so far as it is retributive" (ibid., p. 73).

13. Kant writes that "any undeserved evil that you inflict on someone else among the people is one that you do to yourself. If you vilify him, you vilify yourself; if you steal from him, you steal from yourself; if you kill him, you kill yourself." Since Kant holds that "If what happens to someone is also willed by him, it cannot be a punishment," he takes pains to distance himself from the view that the offender *wills* his punishment. "The chief error contained in this sophistry," Kant writes, "consists in the confusion of the criminal's [that is, the murderer's] own judgment (which one must necessarily attribute to his reason) that he must

forfeit his life with a resolution of the will to take his own life" (Immanuel Kant, *The Metaphysical Elements of Justice, Part I of The Metaphysics of Morals,* trans. by J. Ladd [Indianapolis: Bobbs-Merrill, 1965; originally published in 1797], pp. 101, 105-106). I have tried to capture this notion of attributing a judgment to the offender rather than a resolution of his will with the term 'authorizes.'

14. "Even if a civil society were to dissolve itself by common agreement of all its members . . ., the last murderer remaining in prison must first be executed, so that everyone will duly receive what his actions are worth" (Kant, ibid., p. 102). Interestingly, Conrad calls himself a retributivist, but doesn't accept the strict Kantian version of it. In fact, he claims that Kant "did not bother with justifications for his categorical imperative . . ., [but just] insisted that the Roman *jus talionis* was the reference point at which to begin" (p. 22). Van den Haag, by contrast, states specifically that he is "not a retributivist" (p. 32). In fact he claims that "retributionism" is not really a *theory* of punishment at all, just "a feeling articulated through a metaphor presented as though a theory" (p. 28). This is so, he maintains, because a theory "must tell us what the world, or some part thereof, is like or has been or will be like" (ibid.). "In contrast," he goes on, "deterrence theory is, whether right or wrong, a theory: It asks what the effects are of punishment (does it reduce the crime rate?) and makes testable predictions (punishment reduces the crime rate compared to what it would be without the credible threat of punishment)" (p. 29). Now, it should be obvious that van den Haag has narrowed his conception of "theory" so that it only covers the kind of things one finds in the empirical sciences. So narrowed, there is no such thing as a theory about what justifies some action or policy, no such thing as a Kantian theory of punishment, or, for that matter, a Rawlsian theory of justice—that is to say, no such thing as a *moral* theory. Van den Haag, of course, could use the term 'theory' as he wished, were it not for the fact that he appeals to deterrence theory not merely for predictions about crime rates but also (indeed, in the current context, primarily) as a theory about what justifies punishment—that is, as a *moral* theory. And he must, since the fact that punishment reduces crime does not imply that we should institute punishment unless we *should* do whatever reduces crime. In short, van den Haag is about moral theories the way I am about airplanes: He doesn't quite understand how they work, but he knows how to use them to get where he wants to go.

15. "It may also be pointed out that no one has ever heard of anyone condemned to death on account of murder who complained that he was getting too much [punishment] and therefore was being treated unjustly; everyone would laugh in his face if he were to make such a statement" (Kant, *Metaphysical Elements of Justice,* p. 104; see also p. 133).

16. Herbert Morris defends retributivism on parallel grounds. See his "Persons and Punishment," *The Monist* 52, no. 4 (October 1968):475-501. Isn't what Morris calls "the right to be treated as a person" essentially the right of a rational being to be treated only as he has authorized, implicitly or explicitly, by his own free choices?

17. Bedau writes: "Where criminals set the limits of just methods of punishment, as they will do if we attempt to give exact and literal implementation to *lex talionis,* society will find itself descending to the cruelties and savagery that criminals employ.

But society would be deliberately authorizing such acts, in the cool light of reason, and not (as is often true of vicious criminals) impulsively or in hatred and anger or with an insane or unbalanced mind. Moral restraints, in short, prohibit us from trying to make executions perfectly retributive" (Bedau, "Capital Punishment," p. 176).

18. I am indebted to my colleague Robert Johnson for this suggestion, which he has attempted to develop in "A Life for a Life?" (unpub. ms.). He writes that prisoners condemned to spend their entire lives in prison "would suffer a civil death, the death of freedom. The prison would be their cemetery, a 6' by 9' cell their tomb. Their freedom would be interred in the name of justice. They would be consigned to mark the passages of their lives in the prison's peculiar dead time, which serves no purpose and confers no rewards. In effect, they would give their civil lives in return for the natural lives they have taken."

19. "In the case of homicide, the empirical evidence indicates that poverty and poor economic conditions are systematically related to higher levels of homicide" (Richard M. McGahey, "Dr. Ehrlich's Magic Bullet: Economic Theory, Econometrics, and the Death Penalty," *Crime & Delinquency* 26, no. 4 [October 1980]:502). Some of that evidence can be found in Peter Passell, "The Deterrent Effect of the Death Penalty: A Statistical Test," *Stanford Law Review* (November 1975):61-80.

20. A similar though not identical point has been made by Jeffrie G. Murphy. He writes "I believe that retributivism can be formulated in such a way that it is the only morally defensible theory of punishment. I also believe that arguments, which may be regarded as Marxist at least in spirit, can be formulated which show that social conditions as they obtain in most societies make this form of retributivism largely inapplicable within those societies" (Murphy, "Marxism and Retribution," p. 221). Though my claim here is similar to Murphy's, the route by which I arrive at it differs from his in several ways. Most important, a key point of Murphy's argument is that retributivism assumes that the criminal freely chooses his crime while, according to Murphy, criminals act on the basis of psychological traits that the society has conditioned them to have: "Is it just to punish people who act out of those very motives that society encourages and reinforces? If [Willem] Bonger [a Dutch Marxist criminologist] is correct, much criminality is motivated by greed, selfishness, and indifference to one's fellows; but does not the whole society encourage motives of greed and selfishness ('making it,' 'getting ahead'), and does not the competitive nature of the society alienate men from each other and thereby encourage indifference—even, perhaps, what psychiatrists call psychopathy?" (ibid., p. 239). This argument assumes that the criminal is in some sense unable to conform to legal and moral prohibitions against violence, and thus, like the insane, cannot be thought responsible for his actions. This claim is rather extreme, and dubious as a result. My argument does not claim that criminals, murderers in particular, cannot control their actions. I claim rather that, though criminals can control their actions, when crimes are predictable responses to unjust circumstances, then those who benefit from and do not remedy those conditions bear some responsibility for the crimes and thus the criminals cannot be held *wholly* responsible for them in the sense of being legitimately required to pay their full cost. It should be noted

that Murphy's thesis (quoted at the beginning of this note) is stated in a somewhat confused way. Social conditions that mitigate or eliminate the guilt of offenders do not make retributivism *inapplicable*. Retributivism is applied both when those who are guilty because they freely chose their crimes are punished *and* when it is held wrong to punish those who are not guilty because they did not freely choose their crimes. It is precisely by the application of retributivism that the social conditions referred to by Murphy make the punishment of criminals unjustifiable.

21. Van den Haag notes the connection between crime and poverty, and explains it and its implications as follows: "Poverty," he holds, "does not compel crime; it only makes it more tempting" (p. 207). And it is not absolute poverty that does this, only relative deprivation, the fact that some have less than others (p. 115). In support of this, he marshals data showing that, over the years, crime has risen along with the standard of living at the bottom of society. Since, unlike absolute deprivation, relative deprivation will be with us no matter how rich we all become as long as some have more than others, he concludes that this condition which increases the temptation to crime is just an ineradicable fact of social life, best dealt with by giving people strong incentives to resist the temptation. This argument is flawed in several ways. First, the claim that crime is connected with poverty ought not be simplistically interpreted to mean that a low absolute standard of living itself causes crime. Rather, what seems to be linked to crime is the general breakdown of stable communities, institutions and families, such as has occurred in our cities in recent decades as a result of economic and demographic trends largely out of individuals' control. Of this breakdown, poverty is today a sign and a cause, at least in the sense that poverty leaves people with few defenses against it and few avenues of escape from it. This claim is quite compatible with finding that people with lower absolute standards of living, but who dwell in more stable social surroundings with traditional institutions still intact, have lower crime rates than contemporary poor people who have higher absolute standards of living. Second, the implication of this is not simply that it is relative deprivation that tempts to crime, since if that were the case, the middle class would be stealing as much from the rich as the poor do from the middle class. That this is not the case suggests that there is some threshold after which crime is no longer so tempting, and while this threshold changes historically, it is in principle all one could reach. Thus, it is not merely the (supposedly ineradicable) fact of having less than others that tempts to crime. Finally, everything is altered if the temptation to crime is not the result of an ineradicable social fact, but of an injustice that can be remedied or relieved. Obviously, this would require considerable argument, but it seems to me that the current distribution of wealth in America is unjust whether one takes utilitarianism as one's theory of justice (given the relative numbers of rich and poor in America as well as the principle of declining marginal returns, redistribution could make the poor happier without an offsetting loss in happiness among the rich) or Rawls's theory (the worst-off shares in our society could still be increased, so the difference principle is not yet satisfied) or Nozick's theory (since the original acquisition of property in America was marked by the use of force against Indians and blacks, from which both groups still suffer).

22. In arguing that social injustice disqualifies us from applying the death

penalty, I am arguing that unjust discrimination in the *recruitment* of murderers undermines the justice of applying the penalty under foreseeable conditions in the United States. This is distinct from the argument that points to the discriminatory way in which it has been *applied* to murderers (generally against blacks, particularly when their victims are white). This latter argument is by no means unimportant, nor do I believe that it has been rendered obsolete by the Supreme Court's 1972 decision in *Furman v. Georgia* that struck down then-existing death penalty statutes because they allowed discriminatory application, or the Court's 1976 decision in *Gregg v. Georgia,* which approved several new statutes because they supposedly remedied this problem. There is considerable empirical evidence that much the same pattern of discrimination that led to *Furman* continues after *Gregg.* See for example, William J. Bowers and Glenn L. Pierce, "Arbitrariness and Discrimination in Post-*Furman* Capital Statutes," *Crime & Delinquency* 26, no. 4 (October 1980):563-635. Moreover, I believe that continued evidence of such discrimination would constitute a separate and powerful argument for abolition. Faced with such evidence, van den Haag's strategy is to grant that discrimination is wrong, but claim that it is not "inherent in the death penalty"; it is a characteristic of "its distribution" (p. 206). Thus discrimination is not an objection to the death penalty itself. This rejoinder is unsatisfactory for several reasons. First of all, even if discrimination is not an objection to the death penalty *per se,* its foreseeable persistence is—as the Court recognized in *Furman*—an objection to instituting the death penalty *as a policy.* Moral assessment of the way in which a penalty will be carried out may be distinct from moral assessment of the penalty itself, but, since the way in which the penalty will be carried out is part of what we will be bringing about if we institute the penalty, it is a necessary consideration in any assessment of the morality of instituting the penalty. In short, van den Haag's strategy saves the death penalty in principle, but fails to save it in practice. Second, it may well be that discrimination is (as a matter of social and psychological fact in America) inherent in the penalty of death itself. The evidence of its persistence after *Furman* lends substance to the suspicion that something about the death penalty—perhaps the very terribleness of it that recommends it to van den Haag—strikes at deep-seated racial prejudices in a way that milder penalties do not. In any event, this is an empirical matter, not resolved by analytic distinctions between what is distributed and how it is distributed. Finally, after he mounts his argument against the discrimination objection, van den Haag usually adds that those who oppose capital punishment "because of discriminatory application are not quite serious . . ., [since] they usually will confess, if pressed, that they would continue their opposition even if there were no discrimination whatsoever in the administration of the death penalty" (p. 225). This is preposterous. It assumes that a person can have only one serious objection to any policy. If he had several, then he would naturally continue to oppose the policy *quite seriously* even though all his objections but one were eliminated. In addition to discrimination in the *recruitment* of murderers, and in the *application* of the death penalty among murderers, there is a third sort that affects the justice of instituting the penalty, namely, discrimination in the *legal definition* of murder. I take this and related issues up in *The Rich Get Rich and the Poor Get Prison: Ideology, Class, and Criminal Justice,* 2nd ed. (New York:

John Wiley, 1984).

23. Friedrich Nietzsche, *The Birth of Tragedy and The Genealogy of Morals* (New York: Doubleday, 1956), pp. 199-200.

24. Van den Haag writes that our ancestors "were not as repulsed by physical pain as we are. The change has to do not with our greater smartness or moral superiority but with a new outlook pioneered by the French and American revolutions [namely], the assertion of human equality and with it 'universal identification'], and by such mundane things as the invention of anesthetics, which make pain much less of an everyday experience" (p. 215; cf. van den Haag's *Punishing Criminals* [New York: Basic Books, 1975], pp. 196-206).

25. Emile Durkheim, "Two Laws of Penal Evolution," *Economy and Society* 2 (1973):285 and 294; italics in the original. This essay was originally published in French in *Année* Sociologique 4 (1899-1900). Conrad, incidentally, quotes Durkheim's two laws (p. 39), but does not develop their implications for his side in the debate.

26. Durkheim writes that "of the two laws which we have established, the first contributes to an explanation of the second" (Durkheim, "Two Laws of Penal Evolution," p. 299).

27. The "two causes of the evolution of punishment—the nature of the social type and of the governmental organ—must be carefully distinguished" (ibid., p. 288). Durkheim cites the ancient Hebrews as an example of a society of the less developed type that had milder punishments than societies of the same social type due to the relative absence of absolutist government among the Hebrews (ibid., p. 290).

28. Durkheim's own explanation of the progressive moderation of punishments is somewhat unclear. He rejects the notion that it is due to the growth in sympathy for one's fellows since this, he maintains, would make us more sympathetic with victims and thus harsher in punishments. He argues instead that the trend is due to the shift from understanding crimes as offenses against God (and thus warranting the most terrible of punishments) to understanding them as offenses against men (thus warranting milder punishments). He then seems to come round nearly full circle by maintaining that this shift works to moderate punishments by weakening the religious sentiments that overwhelmed sympathy for the condemned: "The true reason is that the compassion of which the condemned man is the object is no longer overwhelmed by the contrary sentiments which would not let it make itself felt" (ibid., p. 303).

29. Van den Haag seems to waffle on the question of the unique awfulness of execution. For instance, he takes it not to be revolting in the way that earcropping is, because "We all must die. But we must not have our ears cropped" (p. 190), and here he cites John Stuart Mill's parliamentary defense of the death penalty in which Mill maintains that execution only *hastens* death. Mill's point was to defend the claim that "There is not . . . any human infliction which makes an impression on the imagination so entirely out of proportion to its real severity as the punishment of death" (Mill, "Parliamentary Debate," p. 273). And van den Haag seems to agree since he maintains that, since "we cannot imagine our own nonexistence . . ., [t]he fear of the death penalty is in part the fear of the unknown.

It . . . rests on a confusion" (pp. 258-59). On the other hand, he writes that "Execution sharpens our separation anxiety because death becomes clearly foreseen. . . . Further, and perhaps most important, when one is executed he does not just die, he is put to death, forcibly expelled from life. He is told that he is too depraved, unworthy of living with other humans" (p. 258). I think, incidentally, that it is an overstatement to say that we cannot imagine our own nonexistence. If we can imagine any counterfactual experience, for example, how we might feel if we didn't know something that we do in fact know, then it doesn't seem impossible to imagine what it would "feel like" not to live. I think I can arrive at a pretty good approximation of this by trying to imagine how things "felt" to me in the eighteenth century. And, in fact, the sense of the awful difference between being alive and not that enters my experience when I do this, makes the fear of death—not as a state, but as the absence of life—seem hardly to rest on a confusion.

30. I am not here endorsing this view of voluntarily entered slavery or prostitution. I mean only to suggest that it is *the belief* that these relations involve the extreme subjugation of one person to the power of another that is at the basis of their offensiveness. What I am saying is quite compatible with finding that this belief is false with respect to voluntarily entered slavery or prostitution.

31. This is no doubt partly due to modern skepticism about an afterlife. Earlier peoples regarded a foreseen death as a blessing allowing time to make one's peace with God. Writing of the early Middle Ages, Phillippe Aries says, "In this world that was so familiar with death, sudden death was a vile and ugly death; it was frightening; it seemed a strange and monstrous thing that nobody dared talk about" (Phillippe Aries, *The Hour of Our Death* [New York: Vintage, 1982], p. 11).

32. George Orwell, *1984* (New York: American Library, 1983; originally published in 1949), p. 197.

33. I say "might" here to avoid the sticky question of just how effective a deterrent the death penalty would have to be to justify overcoming our scruples about executing. It is here that the other considerations often urged against capital punishment—discrimination, irrevocability, the possibility of mistake, and so on— would play a role. Omitting such qualifications, however, my position might crudely be stated as follows: *Just desert limits what a civilized society may do to deter crime, and deterrence limits what a civilized society may do to give criminals their just deserts.*

34. Isaac Ehrlich, "The Deterrent Effect of Capital Punishment: A Question of Life or Death," *American Economic Review* 65 (June 1975):397-417. For reactions to Ehrlich's work, see Alfred Blumstein, Jacqueline Cohen, and Daniel Nagin, eds., *Deterrence and Incapacitation: Estimating the Effects of Criminal Sanctions on Crime Rates* (Washington, D.C.: National Academy of Sciences, 1978), esp. pp. 59-63 and 336-60; Brian E. Forst, "The Deterrent Effect on Capital Punishment: A Cross-State Analysis," *Minnesota Law Review* 61 (May 1977):743-67, Deryck Beyleveld, "Ehrlich's Analysis of Deterrence," *British Journal of Criminology* 22 (April 1982):101-23, and Isaac Ehrlich, "On Positive Methodology, Ethics and Polemics in Deterrence Research," *British Journal of Criminology* 22 (April 1982):124-39. Much of the criticism of Ehrlich's work focuses on the fact that he found a deterrence impact of executions in the period from 1933-1969, which includes

the period of 1963-1969, a time when hardly any executions were carried out and crime rates rose for reasons that are arguably independent of the existence or nonexistence of capital punishment. When the 1963-1969 period is excluded, no significant deterrence effect shows. Prior to Ehrlich's work, research on the comparative deterrent impact of the death penalty versus life imprisonment indicated no increase in the incidence of homicide in states that abolished the death penalty and no greater incidence of homicide in states without the death penalty compared to similar states with the death penalty. See Thorsten Sellin, *The Death Penalty* (Philadelphia: American Law Institute, 1959).

35. Van den Haag writes: "Other studies published since Ehrlich's contend that his results are due to the techniques and periods he selected, and that different techniques and periods yield different results. Despite a great deal of research on all sides, one cannot say that the statistical evidence is conclusive. Nobody has claimed to have *disproved* that the death penalty may deter more than life imprisonment. But one cannot claim, either, that it has been proved statistically in a conclusive manner that the death penalty does deter more than alternative penalties. This lack of proof does not amount to disproof" (p. 65).

36. An alternative formulation of this "common-sense argument" is put forth and defended by Michael Davis in "Death, Deterrence, and the Method of Common Sense," *Social Theory and Practice* 7, no. 2 (Summer 1981):145-77. Davis's argument is like van den Haag's except that, where van den Haag claims that people *do* fear the death penalty more than lesser penalties and *are* deterred by what they fear most, Davis claims that it is *rational* to fear the death penalty more than lesser penalties and thus *rational* to be more deterred by it. Thus, he concludes that the death penalty is the most effective deterrent *for rational people*. He admits that this argument is "about rational agents, not actual people" (ibid., p. 157). To bring it back to the actual criminal justice system that deals with actual people, Davis claims that the criminal law makes no sense unless we suppose the potential criminal to be (more or less) "rational" (ibid., p. 153). In short, the death penalty is the most effective deterrent because it would be rational to be most effectively deterred by it, and we are committed by belief in the criminal law to supposing that people will do what is rational. The problem with this strategy is that a deterrence justification of a punishment is valid only if it proves that the punishment actually deters actual people from committing crimes. If it doesn't prove that, it misses its mark, no matter what we are committed to supposing. Unless Davis's argument is a way of proving that the actual people governed by the criminal law will be more effectively deterred by the death penalty than by lesser penalties, it is irrelevant to the task at hand. And if it is a way of proving that actual people will be better deterred, then it is indistinguishable from van den Haag's version of the argument and vulnerable to the criticisms of it which follow.

37. David A. Conway writes: "given the choice, I would strongly prefer one thousand years in hell to eternity there. Nonetheless, if one thousand years in hell were the penalty for some action, it would be quite sufficient to deter me from performing that action. The additional years would do nothing to discourage me further. Similarly, the prospect of the death penalty, while worse, may not have any greater deterrent effect than does that of life imprisonment" (David A. Conway,

"Capital Punishment and Deterrence: Some Considerations in Dialogue Form," *Philosophy & Public Affairs* 3, no. 4 [Summer 1974]:433).

38. On the number of people killed by the police, see Lawrence W. Sherman and Robert H. Langworthy, "Measuring Homicide by Police Officers," *Journal of Criminal Law and Criminology* 70, no. 4 (Winter 1979):546-60; on the number of privately owned guns, see Franklin Zimring, *Firearms and Violence in American Life* (Washington, D.C.: U.S. Government Printing Office, 1968), pp. 6-7.

39. *AAA World* (Potomac ed.) 4, no. 3 (May-June 1984), pp. 18c and 18i.

40. A related claim has been made by those who defend the so-called brutalization hypothesis by presenting evidence to show that murders *increase* following an execution. See, for example, William J. Bowers and Glenn L. Pierce, "Deterrence or Brutalization: What is the Effect of Executions?" *Crime & Delinquency* 26, no. 4 (October 1980):453-84. They conclude that each execution gives rise to two additional homicides in the month following, and that these are real additions, not just a change in timing of the homicides (ibid., p. 481). My claim, it should be noted, is not identical to this, since, as I indicate in the text, what I call "the deterrence effect of not executing" is not something whose impact is to be seen immediately following executions but over the long haul, and, further, my claim is compatible with finding no net increase in murders due to executions. Nonetheless, should the brutalization hypothesis be borne out by further studies, it would certainly lend support to the notion that there is a deterrent effect of not executing.

41. Van den Haag writes: "If we were quite ignorant about the marginal deterrent effects of execution, we would have to choose—like it or not—between the certainty of the convicted murderer's death by execution and the likelihood of the survival of future victims of other murderers on the one hand, and on the other his certain survival and the likelihood of the death of new victims. I'd rather execute a man convicted of having murdered others than put the lives of innocents at risk. I find it hard to understand the opposite choice" (p. 69). Conway was able to counter this argument earlier by pointing out that the research on the marginal deterrent effects of execution was not *inconclusive* in the sense of *tending to point both ways,* but rather in the sense of *giving us no reason to believe that capital punishment saves more lives than life imprisonment.* He could then answer van den Haag by saying that the choice is not between risking the lives of murderers and risking the lives of innocents, but between killing a murderer with no reason to believe lives will be saved, and sparing a murderer with no reason to believe lives will be lost (Conway, "Capital Punishment and Deterrence," pp. 442-43). This, of course, makes the choice to spare the murderer more understandable than van den Haag allows. Events, however, have overtaken Conway's argument. The advent of Ehrlich's research, contested though it may be, leaves us in fact with research that tends to point both ways.

Refuting Reiman and Nathanson

Ernest van den Haag

I shall consider Jeffrey Reiman's view of the punishment offenders deserve before turning to his moral scruples, alleged to justify lesser punishments, and to the discriminatory distribution of the death penalty which Stephen Nathanson stresses.

Reiman believes the death penalty is deserved by some murderers, but should never be imposed. Moral scruples should preclude it. If the punishment deserved according to the *lex talionis* is morally repugnant, we may impose less, provided the suffering imposed *in lieu* of what is deserved is proportional to the suffering inflicted on the crime victim. However, suffering exceeding that of his victim can never be deserved by the offender; to impose it would be "unjust for the same reasons that make punishment of the innocent unjust."[1]

MEASUREMENT

How do we know whether the punitive suffering to be imposed on the offender is less or "equal to that which he imposed on the victim" so as not to exceed what he deserves?[2] Cardinal and interpersonal measurement of suffering would be required to find out. Although ordinal measurement is possible in some cases, the cardinal and interpersonal measurement required by Reiman's scheme is not.[3] How many days must the kidnapper be confined, to suffer as much, but no more, than his victim? If he kept his victim three days, are three days of confinement correct? Or three hundred? Or one thousand? If he half-starved his victim, should we do as much to him, or, how do we commute starvation into additional time?

From *Philosophy & Public Affairs* 14, no. 2 (Spring 1985). Copyright © 1985 by Princeton University Press. Reprinted with permission of Princeton University Press.

Punishment for kidnapping can be, within limits, of the same kind as the crime, although all we can actually do to conform to Reiman's prescription even here is to confine for a longer time the kidnapper who kept his victim for a longer time. We have no way of comparing the victim's suffering with the victimizer's, and to limit the latter accordingly. Execution too bears some similarity to the murderer's crime. But confinement? How do we make it commensurate with murder? What about the punishment for assault, burglary, or rape? How do we compare the pain suffered by the victims with the pain to be imposed on the offender by confinement, to make sure that the latter not exceed the former? There is no way of applying Reiman's criterion of desert. Fortunately, we don't need to.

ACTUAL DESERT

Even if, somehow, we knew that three days' confinement inflicts as much pain as his victim suffered on the kidnapper who kept his victim three days, we would feel that the kidnapper deserves much more punishment. That feeling would be appropriate. The offender imposed undeserved suffering on his victim. Why should society not impose undeserved (in Reiman's terminology) suffering on the offender? It would be undeserved only if one accepts Reiman's flawed view of retribution, for, in addition to whatever he deserves for what his victim suffered, the offender also deserves punishment for breaking the law, for imposing undeserved, unlawful suffering on someone. Retributionism of any kind cannot authorize less, despite Reiman's view that suffering imposed on the criminal is unjust when it exceeds the suffering of his victim.

Although occasionally he indicates awareness of the social harm caused by crime and even of the social function of punishment, Reiman treats crimes as though involving but a relationship between victim and offender implemented by judicial authorities.[4] From this faulty premise he infers that retribution should not exceed the harm done to the victim, an idea derived from the *lex talionis*. But that primitive rule was meant to limit the revenge private parties could exact for what was regarded as private harm. The function of the rule was to guard against social disruption by unlimited and indefinitely extended vengeance.

Crimes are no longer regarded merely as private harms. Retribution for the suffering of the individual victims, however much deserved, is not punishment any more than restitution is. Punishment must vindicate the disrupted public order, the violated law, must punish for the social harm done. If my neighbor is burglarized or robbed, he is harmed. But we all must take costly precautions, and we all feel and are threatened: crime harms society as it harms victims. Hence, punishment must, whenever possible, impose pain believed to exceed the pain suffered by the individual victim of crime. No less is deserved. Punishment must be determined by the total gravity of the crime, the social as well as the individual harm, and by the need to deter from the harmful crime. There are ordinal limits to deserved punishments, but cardinal upper limits are set only by harm, habit and sentiment—not by victim suffering.

Let me now turn to the moral scruples which should lead us to reduce punishment to less than what is deserved in some cases. I share some of Reiman's scruples: although he deserves it, I do not want to see the torturer tortured. Other scruples strike me as unjustified.

POVERTY AND CULPABILITY

Reiman believes "that the vast majority of murders in America are a predictable response to the frustrations and disabilities of impoverished social circumstances" which could be, but are not remedied because "others in America benefit," wherefore we have "no right to exact the full cost. . . from our murderers until we have done everything possible to rectify the conditions that produce their crimes."[5] Murder here seems to become the punishment for the sins of the wealthy. According to Reiman, "the vast majority" of current murderers are not fully culpable, since part of the blame for their crimes must be placed on those who fail to "rectify the conditions that produce their crimes."

I grant that certain social conditions predictably produce crime more readily than others. Does it follow that those who commit crimes in criminogenic conditions are less responsible, or blameworthy, than they would be if they did not live in these conditions? Certainly not. Predictability does not reduce responsibility. Reiman remains responsible for his predictable argument. Culpability is reduced only when the criminal's ability to control his actions, or to realize that they are wrong, is abnormally impaired. If not, the social conditions in which the criminal lives have no bearing on his irresponsibility for his acts. Conditions, such as poverty, just or unjust, may increase the temptation to commit crimes. But poverty is neither a necessary nor a sufficient condition for crime, and thus certainly not a coercive one. If there is no compulsion, temptation is no excuse. The law is meant to restrain, and to hold responsible, those tempted to break it. It need not restrain those not tempted, and it cannot restrain those who are unable to control their actions.

Reiman's claim, that even "though criminals can control their actions, when crimes are predictable responses to unjust circumstances, then those who benefit from and do not remedy those conditions bear some responsibility for the crimes and thus the criminals cannot be held *wholly* responsible for them . . ." seems quite unjustified. Those responsible for unjust conditions must be blamed for them,[6] but not for crimes that are "predictable responses to unjust circumstances," if the respondents could have avoided these crimes, as most people living in unjust conditions do.

If crimes are political, that is, address not otherwise remediable "unjust circumstances," they may be held to be morally, if not legally, excusable, on some occasions.[7] But the criminal's moral, let alone legal, responsibility for a crime which he committed for personal gain and could have avoided, is not diminished merely because he lives in unjust circumstances, and his crime was a predictable response to them. Suppose the predictable response to unjust wealth were drunken driving, or rape. Would his wealth excuse the driver or the rapist? Why should poverty, if wealth would not?[8]

Crime is produced by many circumstances, "just" and "unjust." The most just society may have no less crime than the least just (unless "just" is defined circularly as the absence of crime). Tracing crime to causal circumstances is useful and may help us to control it. Suggesting that they *eo ipso* are excuses confuses causality with nonresponsibility. *Tout comprendre ce n'est pas tout pardonner,* Mme. de Staël's followers to the contrary notwithstanding. Excuses require specific circumstances that diminish the actor's control over his actions.

Since "unjust circumstances" do not reduce the responsibility of criminals for their acts, I shall refrain from discussing whether Reiman's circumstances really are unjust, or merely unequal, and whether they do exist because someone benefits from them and could be eliminated if the alleged beneficiaries wished to eliminate them. I am not sure that unjust circumstances always can be remedied, without causing worse injustices. Nor do I share Reiman's confidence that we know what social justice is, or how to produce it.

CIVILIZATION

Reiman thinks that the death penalty is not civilized, because it involves the total subjugation of one person to others, as does slavery, or prostitution.[9]

Whereas slavery usually is not voluntary, the murderer runs the risk of execution voluntarily; he could avoid it by not murdering. I find nothing uncivilized in imposing the risk of subjugation and death on those who decide to murder.

Nota bene: Persons who act with diminished capacity, during moments of passion, are usually convicted of manslaughter rather than murder. Even if convicted of murder, they are not sentenced to death; only if the court believes that the murderer did have a choice, and intended to murder, can he receive the death sentence.

Reiman refers to research finding a brutalization effect, such that executions lead to more homicides. The data are unpersuasive. Some researchers find an increase, some a decrease, of homicides immediately after an execution.[10] Either effect seem ephemeral, involving bunching, rather than changes in the annual homicide rate.

To argue more generally, as Reiman also does, that capital punishment is inconsistent with the advancement of civilization, is to rely on arbitrary definitions of "advancement" and "civilization" for a circular argument. If civilization actually had "advanced" in the direction Reiman, quoting Durkheim, thinks it has, why is that a reason for not preferring "advancement" in some other, perhaps opposite, direction? I cannot find the *moral* (normative) argument in Reiman's description.

DETERRENCE

The death penalty should be retained if abolition would endanger us, Reiman believes. But he does not believe that abolition would. He may be right. However, some of his arguments seem doubtful.

He thinks that whatever marginal deterrent effect capital punishment has, if it has any, is not needed, since life imprisonment provides all the deterrence needed. How can it be ascertained that punishment x deters "everyone who can be deterred" so that punishment x-plus would not deter additional persons? I can see no way to determine this, short of experiments we are unlikely to undertake. Reiman may fear life imprisonment as much, or more, than death. Couldn't someone else fear death more and be insufficiently deterred by life imprisonment?

I cannot prove conclusively that the death penalty deters more than life imprisonment, or that the added deterrence is needed. Reiman cannot prove conclusively that the added deterrence is not needed, or produced. I value the life of innocents more than the life of murderers. Indeed, I value the life of murderers negatively. Wherefore I prefer over- to under-protection. I grant this is a preference.

SELF-DEFENSE

Reiman also believes that murderers who are not deterred by the risk they run because their victims may defend themselves with guns will not be deterred by the risk of execution. This seems unrealistic. Murderers rarely run much risk from self-defense since they usually ambush unsuspecting victims.

TORTURE

On my reasoning, Reiman contends, torture should be used, since it may deter more than execution; or else, even if more deterrent than alternatives, the death penalty should be abolished as torture was: "either we must abolish the electric chair or reinstitute the rack," is his colorful phrase. But there is a difference. I do not oppose torture as undeserved or nondeterrent (although I doubt that the threat of the rack, or of anything adds deterrence to the threat of execution), but simply as repulsive. Death is not; nor is the death penalty. Perhaps repulsiveness is not enough to exclude the rack. If Reiman should convince me that the threat of the rack adds a great deal of deterrence to the threat of execution he might persuade me to overcome my revulsion and to favor the rack as well. It certainly can be deserved.

MORAL THEORY

In *The Death Penalty: A Debate*[11] I noted that only when punishments are based not on retribution alone, but also on deterrence, they rest on a theory, that is, on a correlation of recurrent facts to a prediction: punishment x will, *ceteris paribus,* reduce the rate of crime y by 10%, and x-plus will bring a reduction of 20%. Reiman censures me for using "theory" when I should have written "empirical theory." He is right. Further, deterrence does not morally justify any punishment, unless one has first accepted the moral desirability of reducing crime, and the tolerability of the costs. I should have pointed that out. Finally, I did not mean to deny that there are moral theories to justify retribution. They strike me as more dependent on feeling than empirical theories are. More to the point, unlike deterrence theory, justice theories are not meant to predict the effect of various punishments, and are not capable of determining, except ordinally, what these punishments should be, although they can help to justify the distribution of punishments.[12]

MODES OF EXECUTION

As Reiman stresses, the spectacle of execution is not pretty. Nor is surgery. Wherefore both should be attended only by the necessary personnel.[13] I do not find Reiman's aesthetic or moral scruples sufficient to preclude execution or surgery. However, I share his view that lethal injections are particularly unpleasant, not so much because of the subjugation which disturbs him, but because of the veterinary air. (We put animals "to sleep" when sick or inconvenient.) In contrast, shooting strikes me as dignified; it is painless too and probably the best way of doing what is necessary.

LIFE IMPRISONMENT

Reiman proposes life imprisonment without parole instead of execution. Although less feared, and therefore likely to be less deterrent, actual lifelong imprisonment strikes me as more cruel than execution even if perceived as less harsh. Its comparative cruelty was stressed already by Cesare Bonesana, Marchese di Beccaria, and by many other since.

Life imprisonment also becomes undeserved over time. A person who committed a murder when twenty years old and is executed within five years—far too long and cruel a delay in my opinion—is, when executed, still the person who committed the crime for which he is punished. His identity changes little in five years. However, a person who committed a murder when he was twenty years old and is kept in prison when sixty years old, is no longer the same person who committed the crime for which he is still being punished. The sexagenarian is unlikely to have much in common with the twenty-year-old for whose act he is being punished; his legal identity no longer reflects reality. Personality and actual identity are not that continuous. In effect, we punish an innocent sexagenarian who does not deserve punishment, instead of a guilty twenty-year-old who did. This spectacle should offend our moral sensibilities more than the deserved execution of the twenty-year-old. Those who deserve the death penalty should be executed while they deserve it, not kept in prison when they no longer deserve any punishment.

DISCRIMINATION

Disagreeing with the Supreme Court, Stephen Nathanson believes that the death penalty still is distributed in an excessively capricious and discriminatory manner. He thinks capital punishment is "unjust" because poor blacks are more likely to be sentenced to death than wealthy whites. Further, blacks who murdered whites are more likely to be executed than those who murdered blacks.[14] This last discrimination has been thrown into relief recently by authors who seem to be under the impression that they have revealed a new form of discrimination against black murderers. They have not. The practice invidiously discriminates against black victims of murder, who are not as fully, or as often, vindicated as white victims are. However, discrimination against a class of victims, although invidious enough, does not amount to discrimination against their victimizers. The discrimination against black victims, the lesser punishment given their murderers, actually favors black murderers, since most black victims are killed by black murderers. Stephen Nathanson and Jeffrey Reiman appear to think that they have captured additional discrimination against black defendants. They are wrong.

Neither the argument from discrimination against black victims, nor the argument from discrimination against black murderers, has any bearing on the guilt of black murderers, or on the punishment they deserve.

Invidious discrimination is never defensible. Yet I do not see wherein it, in Reiman's words, "would constitute a separate and powerful argument for abolition," or does make the death penalty "unjust" for those discriminatorily selected to suffer it, as Stephen Nathanson believes.[15] If we grant that some (even all) murderers of blacks, or, some (even all) white and rich murderers, escape the death penalty, how does that reduce the guilt of murderers of whites, or of black and poor murderers, so that they should be spared execution too? Guilt is personal. No murderer becomes less guilty, or less deserving of punishment, because another murderer was punished leniently, or escaped punishment altogether. We should try our best to bring every murderer to justice. But if one got away with murder wherein is that a reason to let anyone else get away? A group of murderers does not become less deserving of punishment because another equally guilty group is not punished, or punished less. We can punish only a very small proportion of all criminals. Unavoidably they are selected accidentally. We should reduce this accidentality as much as possible but we cannot eliminate it.[16]

EQUAL INJUSTICE AND UNEQUAL JUSTICE

Reiman and Nathanson appear to prefer equal injustice—letting all get away with murder if some do—to unequal justice: punishing some guilty offenders according to desert, even if others get away. Equal justice is best, but unattainable. Unequal justice is our lot in this world. It is the only justice we can ever have, for not all murderers can be apprehended or convicted, or sentenced equally in different courts. We should constantly try to bring every offender to justice. But meanwhile unequal justice is the only justice we have, and certainly better than equal injustice—giving no murderer the punishment his crime deserves.

MORE DISCRIMINATION

Nathanson insists that some arbitrary selections among those equally guilty are not "just." He thinks that selecting only bearded speeders for ticketing, allowing the cleanshaven to escape, is unjust. Yet the punishment of the bearded speeders is not unjust. The escape of the cleanshaven ones is. I never maintained that a discriminatory distribution is just—only that it is irrelevant to the guilt and deserved punishment of those actually guilty.

Nathanson further suggests that it is not just to spare some student plagiarizers punishment for (I suppose) irrelevant reasons, while punishing others. Again the distribution is discriminatory, i.e., unjust. But the punishment of the plagiarizers selected is not. (The non-punishment of the others is.) Nathanson thinks that giving a prize only to one of three deserving children (his own) is unjust. Not to the deserving child. Only to the others, just as it was unjust not to punish the others who deserved it, but not unjust to punish the deserving plagiarizers who were irrelevantly selected.[17]

Nathanson taxes me with inconsistency because in a footnote I wrote that irrelevant discriminations are "not acceptable to our sense of justice." They are not. But I did not say that those who deserved the punishment received, or the reward, were unjustly treated, that is, did not deserve it and should not have received it. Rather those equally situated also should have received it, and the distribution was offensive because they did not. Whenever possible this inequality should be corrected, but certainly not by not distributing the punishment, or the reward at issue, or by not giving it to the deserving. Rather by giving it as well to those who because of discrimination did not get it. (I might have done better to write in my footnote that discriminatory distributions offend our sense of *equal* justice. But neither the Constitution nor I favor replacing justice with equality.)

Nathanson quotes the late Justice Douglas suggesting that a law which deliberately prescribes execution only for the guilty poor, or which has that effect, would be unconstitutional. Perhaps. But the vice would be in exempting the guilty rich; the guilty poor would remain guilty, and deserving of prescribed punishment even if the guilty rich escape legally or otherwise.[18]

Further on Nathanson points out that the inevitable capriciousness in the distribution of punishments (only a very small percentage of offenders are ever punished and the selection unavoidably is morally arbitrary) while no reason to abolish punishment in general, may still be an argument for abolishing capital punishment because of its unique severity, and because we could survive without. We can survive without many things, which is not reason for doing without, if one thinks, as I do, that we survive *better* with. As for the unique severity of the death penalty it is, of course, the reason for imposing it for uniquely heinous crimes. The guilt of those who committed them is not diminished, if they are selected by a lottery from among all those guilty of the crime.

Following Charles Black, Nathanson notes that those executed are not necessarily the worst murderers, since there is no way of selecting these. He is right. It seems quite sufficient, however, that those executed, though not the worst, are bad enough to deserve execution. That others who deserved it even more got away, does not make those executed insufficiently deserving.

Nathanson goes on to insist that "not every person who kills another is guilty of the same crime." True. Wherefore the law makes many distinctions, leaving only a small group of those guilty of homicide eligible for the death penalty. Further, capital punishment is not mandated. The court must decide in each case whether or not to impose it. To impose capital punishment, courts must find that the aggravating circumstances attending the murder outweigh the mitigating ones, both of which must be listed in the law. Nathanson is right in pointing out that the criteria listed in the law are not easy to apply. If they were, we would not need the judgment of the court. That judgment is not easy to make. It may seem too severe, or not severe enough, in some cases, as would mandated penalties. So what else is new?

NOTES

1. See Jeffrey H. Reiman, "Justice, Civilization, and the Death Penalty: Answering van den Haag," *Philosophy & Public Affairs* 14, no. 2: 128. Unless otherwise noted, all my quotations are taken from Reiman's article.

2. This question arises only when the literal *lex talionis* is abandoned—as Reiman proposes to do, for good reason—in favor of the proportional retribution he suggests. How, by the way, would we punish a skyjacker? Summing up the suffering of all the skyjacked passengers? What about the damage to air traffic?

3. The order of punishments is notoriously hard to coordinate with the order of crimes; even when punishments are homogeneous, crimes are not.

4. Perhaps Reiman's excessive reliance on the Hegelian justification of retribution (to vindicate the equality of victim and offender) or on the Kantian version (to vindicate the rationality of both) is to blame.

5. Reiman does not say here that murder deserves less than the death penalty, but only that "the vast majority of murderers" deserve less because impoverished. However, wealthy murderers can be fully culpable, so that we may "exact the full cost" from them.

6. Who are they? They are not necessarily the beneficiaries, as Reiman appears to believe. I benefit from rent control, which I think unjust to my landlord, but I'm not responsible for it. I may benefit from low prices for services or goods, without being responsible for them, or for predictable criminal responses to them. Criminals benefit from the unjust exclusionary rules of our courts. Are they to blame for these rules?

7. See my *Political Violence & Civil Disobedience, passim* (New York: Harper & Row, 1972) for a more detailed argument.

8. Suppose unjust wealth tends to corrupt, and unjust poverty does not.

Would the wealthy be less to blame for their crimes?

9. Prostitution does not involve total subjugation and is voluntary. In an ambiguous footnote Reiman asserts that it is the perception of prostitution as subjugation that makes it offensive. But this perception, derived from pulp novels more than from reality, is not what makes the voluntary act offensive. Rather, it is the sale of sex as a fungible service, divorced from affection and depersonalized that is offensive. Anyway, when something is offensive because misperceived it is not the thing that is offensive.

10. David P. Phillips, "The Deterrent Effect of Capital Punishment: New Evidence on an Old Controversy," *The American Journal of Sociology* (July 1980). For further discussion see loc. cit., July 1982. See also Lester, *Executions as a Deterrent to Homicides,* 44 *Psychological Rep.* 562 (1979).

11. Ernest van den Haag and John P. Conrad (New York: Plenum Press, 1983).

12. See my *Punishing Criminals* (New York: Basic Books, 1975) which is superseded to some extent by the views expressed in my "Criminal Law as a Threat System," 73 *Journal of Criminal Law and Criminology* 2 (1982).

13. Both spectacles when graphically shown may also give rise to undesirable imitations or inspirations.

14. Despite some doubts, I am here granting the truth of both hypotheses.

15. Stephen Nathanson, "Does It Matter if the Death Penalty Is Arbitrarily Administered?" *Philosophy & Public Affairs* 14, no. 2 (this issue). Unless otherwise noted, all further quotations are taken from Nathanson's article.

16. Discrimination or capriciousness is (when thought to be avoidable and excessive) sometimes allowed by the courts as a defense. Apparently this legal device is meant to reduce discrimination and capriciousness. But those spared because selected discriminatorily for punishment do not become any less deserving of it as both Reiman and Nathanson think, although not punishing them is used as a means to foster the desired equality in the distributions of punishments.

17. There will be some difficulty in explaining to the children who did not get the reward, why they did not, but no difficulty in explaining why one deserving child got it—unless the children share Nathanson's difficulty in distinguishing between justice and equality.

18. See footnote 16.